School of Divinity

Gardner-Webb University
School of Divinity

This book donated
by

Rev. Charles Rabon

FINDING GOD ON THE A TRAIN

FINDING GOD ON THE Ⓐ TRAIN

A Journey into Prayer

RICK HAMLIN

HarperSanFrancisco
An Imprint of HarperCollins*Publishers*

FINDING GOD ON THE A TRAIN: *A Journey into Prayer.* Copyright © 1997 by
Rick Hamlin. All rights reserved. Printed in the United States of America.
No part of this book may be used or reproduced in any manner whatsoever
without written permission except in the case of brief quotations embodied
in critical articles and reviews. For information address HarperCollins
Publishers, 10 East 53rd Street, New York, NY 10022.
HarperCollins Web Site: http://www.harpercollins.com
HarperCollins®, 🐟®, and HarperSanFrancisco™ are trademarks of
HarperCollins Publishers Inc.

FIRST EDITION

Library of Congress Cataloging-in-Publication Data
Hamlin, Rick.
Finding god on the A train : a journey into prayer / Rick Hamlin.
ISBN 0–06–063596–7 (cloth)
ISBN 0–06–063597–5 (pbk.)
1. Prayer—Christianity. 2. Hamlin, Rick. I. Title.
BV215.H34   1996
248.3'2—dc20   96–28206
97 98 99 00 ICC\RRD-H 10 9 8 7 6 5 4 3 2

For Sweetie

This book wouldn't have happened without the encouragement and help of many. I'm especially grateful to Abraham Feldman for his careful reading of the manuscript, to Elizabeth Sherrill for her wise editorial suggestions, to my wife, Carol Wallace, who knows exactly when a word is right. I'm indebted to my Guideposts colleagues, who have taught me as much (or as little) as I know about inspirational writing. I've been flattered by their enthusiasm for this book, and I'd like to single out my editor-in-chief, Fulton Oursler, for his support and Elizabeth Gold and Brigitte Weeks for their book-world knowledge.

Of course, I wouldn't have had a story to tell without spiritual directors, even under other titles. Thank you Arthur Caliandro, Susan Harriss, Fred Hill, Florence Pert, Tom Pike, Ken Ruge, Rick Thyne. I've been greatly helped by others who have written about prayer, especially Frederick Buechner, Larry Dossey, Harry Emerson Fosdick, Morton Kelsey, C. S. Lewis, Arnold Prater. My prayer-breakfast friends have heard about this project for a long time, and I don't doubt that their prayers and those of many others helped make it happen. My own prayers have often been for Claire Townsend, who read and commented on this book only weeks before she died.

But the person who most constantly prodded me along the way was Fred Bernstein. Several years ago he said, "Tell me why you think prayer is important," and he wouldn't give up until he read this manuscript and made sure others saw it. I hope when he reads this, as surely he will, he will forgo his usual modesty and take the well-deserved credit.

This is my place. This is my time. This is my discipline.

The subway rattles, shakes, and rolls. The tabloid headlines scream out in bold black letters, diverting my attention. Who was killed? Who was maimed? Who won the ballgame? The kids sitting next to me and standing above me are talking about school. One poor lone soul in baggy pants with the crotch at his knees is doing his homework, scratching the answers to algebraic equations in a workbook while trying to contribute to the conversation around him about girlfriends and teachers and music. Others have music plugged in their ears. Very loud. It sounds like rap, but all I get from where I sit is rhythm and bass.

At least the kids are easier to ignore than the old people. Old people standing on a crowded subway while I sit are the worst distraction of all. Old people who get on at 168th Street or 145th Street after I've settled into one of the few seats. Old people who can barely reach the metal straps that hang above my head. I hear their sighs. I feel their packages at my toes. Looking down, I can see their tired feet, the women in hose that bunch at the ankles. I avoid looking up, wary of meeting the gaze that will say, "Give me your seat, please." I avoid noticing how old they are by focusing on the small book in my lap or closing my eyes and thinking about God.

This is my place. This is my time. And if I really believed in the integrity of this devotional time, I would get up and offer my place to someone who probably deserves it more than I do. But that would mean stopping my prayer time for a moment, leaving off the meditation that I desperately crave. But I already have stopped. There's no choice. I look up and lock eyes. I offer my seat. The woman shakes her head no. I insist. She nods again. She says something to me in Spanish and indicates by her gestures that she doesn't mind standing. I look at what she's reading. I can make out a few words about God and prayer. I smile. This is her place too. We're not alone. *Where two or three are gathered together in my name, there am I in the midst of them.*

I close my eyes again and concentrate. Without even gazing around, I know there are others here too. I've come to know them by sight over the years. There's the woman with the red chapped hands who takes a rosary out of her frayed overcoat pocket and fingers the beads with one hand while holding on to a pole with the other (unless she, the fortunate one, has found a place to sit). There's the young Orthodox Jewish man with a thin brown beard barely covering his pink cheeks and chin. His prayer book is a mystery to me, the pages going back to front, the words right to left. There are Bible readers with black, well-thumbed books, passages circled and underlined in multicolored ink. I avoid their eyes because when they see what I'm reading they invite me to their neighborhood Bible study groups, and although I admire their commitment, this morning I don't want to hear their textual analysis. I don't even want to hear their witness, however moving their tales might be. This is not my time for community—except for the silent community that we create as we pray separately together on our journey south to make money for mortgages, rent, groceries, spouses and children, pizza and a movie on Saturday night.

Despite my best antisocial efforts, someone I know sits down next to me and I have to talk. My neighbor and I happen to find ourselves on the same train, in the same car, on the same bench, and although I can tell that he'd rather read the newspaper folded open in his hands and I'd rather look at the book in my lap, we make conversation. Of course, we could avoid talking about anything important by sticking to the weather, and then he could wander back to the front page and (if I proved brave enough to expose my fumbling efforts at faith) I might stray back to this little green-bound pocket edition of the New Testament and psalms.

Instead, we connect. We discuss a mutual friend who's seriously ill. We talk about frustrations we have as parents of boys who are close in age. "How's your son doing in soccer this year?" "Is he planning to do baseball in the spring?" "What do you do when he doesn't do his homework?" We share our love of community and discuss the odd, awkward way our apartment building makes us a community.

At 59th Street, where we both get off the A express train— he goes upstairs to take another train and I wait for the local— we bid each other good-bye. How much time did we spend together? Twenty minutes at the most. But the time wasn't wasted. We'e good friends. We exchanged news and advice. We talked. And as much as I'd dreaded the interruption of the business I'd set out to accomplish, I was grateful for it in the end.

"The Holy Spirit is the Lord of our time," a minister once said to me when we were discussing time management and how frustrating it was that you could never get done exactly what you planned to get done. "We give ourselves goals, deadlines, schedules, timetables," he explained, "but in the end, the Holy Spirit is the Lord of our time." I understood what he meant. The interruptions—the problem phone call, the crisis at home, the sick colleague whose job we must fill—are holy obligations as serious as the devotional time we've set aside to be with God. *Therefore if thou bring thy gift to the altar, and there rememberest that thy brother hath ought against thee; Leave there thy gift before the altar, and go thy way; first be reconciled to thy brother, and then come and offer thy gift.*

So morning after morning I come to this place in a world of distractions, and I pray. I don't clock myself, but I use the subway stops as markers, guiding me in my ritual. I read from the 181st Street station to the 125th Street station, usually from the Bible, occasionally from what my wife calls a "God book"—a work by some metaphysical sage, recent or not so recent. Then at 125th Street I close my eyes. It's the express train, no more stops from there to 59th Street. At least five minutes (but as I say, I've never clocked it) of uninterrupted time. This is my time for God.

It's so little. I'm almost ashamed to admit to it on paper. There are other times too, I hasten to add. There are spot prayers uttered at work between taking a telephone call, making a trip to the water cooler, and wrestling with movable icons on the computer. There are letters that are really prayers as they capture a wish or a dream or a hope for someone else. There are formal prayers said at church on my knees, or grace at dinner with the children, thanking God for the minutiae of a day. There are those prayers I say in bed at night when I can't get to sleep because of worries about friends or work or family. And then there are songs that are prayers lingering in my head like the incense that clings to my jacket after a High Church festival Sunday with the thurifer swinging the billowing censer while smoke-sensitive choir members cover their mouths with handkerchiefs.

But this early-morning time of prayer feels like the most important. Without it my day would fall apart and I would forget whose I am and what I want to do and what I believe. It's the time without which I would exist only for myself, without which I would be consumed by petty demands on my time and petty distractions of my ego. I would be pulled into a thousand pieces by the various roles of life I play—friend, singer, son, do-gooder, student, worshiper, committee member, faithful correspondent, telephone talker, writer, editor, husband, father.

It's my time. It's my place.

It all started about a dozen years ago, but I can think of a better place to start. Something my mother made me do when I was very young.

I was the third of four children. We were evenly spaced out, two years apart: girl, boy, boy, girl. We were raised in Southern California in the fifties and sixties. Whenever I see one of those family movies or classic TV sitcoms of the period, I'm briefly reminded of the world I grew up in. The people look and sound like sanitized versions of the neighbors I knew, the kids playing sandlot baseball on the cul-de-sac, the mothers hanging up laundry and gossiping over the back fence, morning newspapers arriving on the front porch and prize petunias blooming in back. The block on *Hazel* or *Leave It to Beaver* or *Ozzie and Harriet* could have been my block with its neat sidewalks, clipped hedges, cheerful green lawns, and open carports, illuminated by the bright, overexposed, yellowy sunlight of the L.A. Basin on a smoggy day.

I lived on a street that had been named by my grandfather when he lived in the neo-Spanish tiled house that dominated the block. That's where my mother was born. Then, a generation later, my grandfather built our one-story modern house behind a row of stucco tract homes. Next door was a vacant lot filled every winter with towering mustard weed that we used for making forts (making it easy to picture in Sunday school the startling scale of what comes from faith as small as a mustard seed). In the gully below our house ran a dry riverbed that had been covered over with cement so that it would take the runoff from hoses, sprinklers, and winter rains to the sea.

Dad worked as a salesman in my youngest days. He took long road trips up the Central Valley selling farm machinery and then flew back to the Midwest to visit the manufacturers he represented. Mom was often left on her own to rear her four children, and all told she did a good job. Especially when you consider that she herself had been reared by nannies, housekeepers, and a nervous neo-Victorian mother who was capable of warmth but no great spontaneity. My mother's mother lived for her regular games of golf and bridge at the country club. She was hopeless in the nursery or the kitchen. She actually had a nervous breakdown after my mother was born and took off to Europe for months to recover, leaving the children behind. So in many ways Mom started from scratch with us. And what she couldn't intuit she gathered from the popular advice dispensed in paperbacks and magazines.

In one of those publications, about the time I was born, Mom read an article suggesting that children needed time to be by themselves. Not just naptime or bedtime, but time during the day when a child could be behind a closed door (left slightly ajar, should the child call for help), sitting on a bed, gazing at the pages of a book or running a miniature car around a track on the chenille bedspread. With four energetic children, Mom appreciated the wisdom of advice that would allow her a few moments away from us. Once we were settled, she retreated to her bedroom for solitude. During hot September days when the Santa Ana winds blew from the desert, I remember her even resting in the bathroom. Given the lack of air-conditioning in our house, the white tile floor of that room was the coolest place around.

Many of my recollections from early childhood are images from this mandated rest time. I can remember looking out across the brick patio in the back to my brother's ramshackle treehouse. I can hear the sound of trucks driving on the main street that lay beyond the yellowing field of mustard. Sometimes I can hear the distant whistle of a train on the tracks that skirted our town's historic adobe mission. In midafternoon I can feel the heat of the sun melting my crayons as it shone through the large picture windows that looked out over the gully down to the concrete riverbed. But one of my key recollections isn't even from home.

We were at my grandparents' beach house. It sat high on a hill surrounded by ice plant and pink and white geraniums that gave off a bitter smell when we stepped on them. From the front we walked down a wooden path that snaked down the cliff to the surging Pacific. Waves pounded on the rock-strewn beach, carving out caves in the cliffs and bringing kelp to the sand. I didn't like to be on the beach, even when an adult held my hand. I found the water itself frightening and the noise of the waves terrifying. But from up on the cliff, looking down, I loved staring at the water.

That afternoon of my vivid memory I was in an upstairs bedroom for my twenty minutes alone. I crept up to the large

plate-glass window, tinted green to keep out the glare, and I
looked down to the lawn, the wooden chaise lounge draped
with wet beach towels, the plastic bucket and shovel awaiting
my return. Down the slope and beyond the sand and rock, the
kelp beds sloshed up and down in the ocean like my mother's
nylon stockings being washed in the kitchen sink. The waves
rolled slowly, and the wind blew whitecaps across the tops.
The sea stretched endlessly, going as far as the eye could see,
finally disappearing in the haze of a gray fogbank. What had
frightened me close-up now took on the luster of magic, the
sunlight sparkling on the water like glitter spilled from a bottle
or sequins on a majorette's gown in the Rose Parade.

As the wind blew and the waves rolled, I squinted, breaking
the reflected light into a rainbow's prism. How long I stood
there and gazed I don't know. Time stopped. I was left alone.
If children are lost in thought, leave them be. That was my
mother's blessing. It was a wonderful gift. She taught me how
to love being by myself. She showed me what wonderful dis-
coveries I could make on my own.

First there was the initial boredom. Then a moment of
panic: "What if I don't have anything to do?" (I still get stuck at
this step. I rush out of the house with a satchel overloaded
with books and magazines for fear of an unfilled hour. Time
lost. "Lost, yesterday, somewhere between sunrise and sunset,
two golden hours, each set with sixty diamond minutes. No re-
ward is offered, for they are gone forever," said Horace Mann.
Victorian nonsense I still seem to live by.) Then, if I allowed
myself to relax, I would rest silent and make friends of solitude. I would look with the inner eye and listen to the inner

voice. My imagination opened up. Stories came to mind. A crack in the plaster ceiling took on shape. The rhythm of a rope flapping against the flagpole sounded the first notes of a symphony. It was my time, my time alone.

So prayer, when it was reintroduced to me, found fertile ground. I was used to listening to my soul. I'd discovered how solitude brought comfort that could be lost in the haranguing crowd. And at an early age I was given a solid sense of self that I kept with me so that I could disappear from the world (while still being in the world) and discover an inner world.

What a lost Eden! What an easy thing to allow to slip through your fingers! For it has come and gone and then come back to me. But I must never forget. Solitude has been my source of strength throughout the years, even in its most basic form, even without addressing a Supreme Being. I need to take time alone.

"Take time every day" was the advice of the man who set me on this spiritual journey a dozen years ago. I met him in his home office in his New York apartment, a room with dark-green walls, Oriental rugs, a cordovan sofa, wing chairs, and framed prints of the Holy Land done by nineteenth-century landscape painters. We met first thing in the morning, before work and after his church's morning prayer service. His wife usually left him some toast and marmalade on a silver tray and he ate as we talked—or rather *he* talked. He always offered me a piece of the toast with marmalade, which I ate hungrily.

He made me nervous because his eyes often wandered during our morning sessions: to his phone, which illuminated if anyone was on another line, to the view of treetops outside his window, to the well-worn books on the shelves that revealed his erudition, to the closed paneled doors. Behind those doors his family could be heard getting ready for the day. Did he listen to me? Or was he listening to his son complaining about having to wear a jacket on such a warm day and the baby-sitter receiving her marching orders and his wife fielding a call from a parishioner? And then just when I thought he hadn't heard a word I said, he turned his blue eyes on me and asked a perceptive question that showed he had followed every phrase.

He was a minister, and that was why I had been sent to him. A friend of a friend, he professed to be interested in my spiritual plight. I was not of his parish, I was not of his denomination, but at the recommendation of our mutual friend, I found myself in his office, studying the frayed threads of the Oriental rugs while his wandering gaze sometimes lingered on me.

"Do you know God?" he asked at our first session, not wasting any time.

"Do I what?"

"Do you know God?" he repeated. "You've got to be able to answer that question first."

It was the worst possible question, and it took me completely off guard. I didn't expect it of him. Partly because he was of that nice blue-blooded ministerial stock, Yale U. and Div. School, which seems more concerned with preserving the church's architectural heritage—shoring up buttresses and keeping dry rot out of the beams—than knowing God. He had the right society minister's looks: tall, tanned, rugged, and handsome, making a clerical collar the ultimate fashionable accessory, like a pectoral cross on a runway model. I had expected some fancy theological talk about a Higher Power and maybe a copy of Reinhold Niebuhr shoved across the table to me. To speak so frankly about faith, even for a minister, seemed in the worst of taste.

"I grew up going to church," I said, or something like that. I'd gone to Sunday school, I'd sung in choirs, I'd been baptized, . . . and at the appropriate age, I'd joined the church. Because I came at the tail end of the Right On generation, the end of the baby boomers, I had participated in church-sponsored peace rallies and marches to end world hunger. I had stayed up late in church basement coffee houses and had passed around petitions in favor of getting the United States out of Vietnam. I'd grown up in a congregation that was hip enough to have a bearded youth minister who rode a motorcycle and strummed a guitar, singing folk songs about the martyrdom of Abraham, Martin, and John. I'd sat through sensitive rap sessions in that same church basement, as we lounged on batik-print pillows around scented candles, talking about how friendship was like a bridge over troubled water. And I'd been in youth services of contemporary worship where we passed out daisies and danced before the altar.

But did I know God?

As his eyes wandered, I told him that I was still a church-goer, was even paid for it because I had a decent tenor voice (and in New York City if you had a good enough voice and could read music, you could get a Sunday job as a paid chorister). I didn't have to admit I was in church to find out more about God. It was a job. It was money. It was a small check every month.

He grabbed a piece of toast off the sterling-silver platter. He probably had a dozen things on his mind. A meeting with the ladies from the Altar Guild, a sermon to write, a hospital to visit? And I searched my mind for something to say.

The only analogy I could come up with was that if I knew God, it was the way you knew the parents of your best friend from high school. You'd been in their house hundreds of times (although not in their bedroom), and whenever you saw them, they asked you polite questions about what college you hoped to attend and what you wanted to study and what you wanted to be when you grew up, but no matter how often they insisted upon it, you couldn't bring yourself to call them by their first names.

"No, I don't really know God," I said after a time.

"You don't know God?" he repeated.

"I suppose I don't."

"Do you want to know him?"

"Yes. That's why I'm here."

"Good. Well, here's what you must do." He turned to me, his attention focused. Now I felt it coming, the salesman's canned spiel, the well-rehearsed pitch. He would give me some stapled pamphlet with stick-figure drawings and time-worn phrases. He would tell me the steps I needed to follow— one, two, three, four, five—and at the end he'd put one clammy hand on my head and ask me to open my heart.

Instead, he dusted the toast crumbs off his fingers and licked a swirl of marmalade from his thumb. "You must pray every day," he said. "Five minutes or an hour—it doesn't really matter how long. What's important is that you do it every day, even when you don't think you have anything to say. *God* will have something to say. Get yourself to a private place and pray."

"Should I read the Bible?"

"That would probably help."

"Should I get down on my knees?"

"If you'd like."

"Should I find a group of other people to pray with?"

"That can be a good idea."

I was asking questions simply to prolong the discussion, but he stood up to indicate that our session was over. He expected to see me again. He would be my spiritual director—that was the term he used. He would be glad to guide me in my exploration. Now the ball was in my court.

He prayed over me, brisk, godly words, and then gave me a bear hug, a warm gesture that took me by surprise. He stood back and smiled. I was free to go. No charge. It wasn't like a visit with a therapist. We would meet again. He turned to a page in his pocket calendar. Two weeks from now? Fine. Same time? Great.

The next morning, before the winter sunrise, I went into the office of our one-bedroom Upper Westside brownstone apartment and opened the Bible to a few psalms. I had set the alarm so I'd be sure to have enough time before the day began. But I woke up on my own at 6:30 on the dot, as alert as though I were about to leave for a jet trip across the country. I had that sense of anticipation you have before making a long journey. The bags packed, the plants watered, the refrigerator empty.

I will lift up mine eyes unto the hills, from whence cometh my help.

I didn't kneel. It would have made me too self-conscious. I closed my eyes and kept my hands on the Bible.

My help cometh from the Lord, which made heaven and earth.

I heard the radiator rattle and someone flush a toilet in the apartment one floor beneath us, the water surging through the pipes. I heard my wife pull the covers tighter around her on the futon on the floor in the next room. I heard the refrigerator switch on, the lights dimming slightly from the loss of power. I could hear my own breathing. What was there to say?

Inspired by the Bible, I reached for some exalted phrases. I could think of a few sick people to pray for. A friend's mother had cancer; another friend's grandfather was having open-heart surgery. And I knew plenty of people with money woes; I could pray for them. I could pray for my wife, Carol, and the book she was writing. And peace, I could pray for peace. But what did I really want with God? What did I want to say?

In the silence, in the old house's creaking and groaning as it woke up, something came to me. First a nothingness, as though I were a blank slate waiting to be filled. Then an uneasy feeling inside, like the gurgling I heard in the water pipes behind the walls. Finally a question as shaming as the anxiety that comes before entering a room full of strangers at a party: Would God have anything to say to me?

CHAPTER

Those first mornings in our apartment's office, as I thumbed through the psalms in my small pocket Bible and looked for God, I found gnawing evidence of my own inadequacy. The silence told me how little I liked myself, and as I kept telling God I wanted to serve him somehow, I felt very small. Would my life ever count for something? What did God want of me? Surely he must exist, for he was the only one who could help me. I felt so low that getting on my hands and knees and crawling under the desk would have suited me fine. Was this what it was to know God? I wasn't sure I liked it. And all those psalms. What was so exalting about their phrases? *I am a worm and no man. . . . Why do the heathen rage? Break thou the arm of the wicked and the evil man.* Nothing nice and sweet. Nothing pious and churchy.

I would have given up early in this pilgrimage but for my deep need and two things I had learned about myself.

First there was something I had discovered in my writing. During the first year of my marriage I was working at being a writer. That was my principal occupation. Every day, after prayer, after doing the breakfast dishes, I wrote.

Like all struggling writers, I had turned to the works of other, greater writers for inspiration and advice. At the time I

had written an (unpublished) murder mystery. As a native Californian and Angeleno romantic, I read a lot of Raymond
Chandler. I couldn't imagine writing as well as he did. I made
my way through his novels and then, still searching for some
clue to how he worked, read a volume of his letters, a book I
found on the shelf of my mother-in-law's home. Somewhere
in a letter to a would-be writer he had this wise thing to say
about writing fiction (I paraphrase):

*If you want to be a writer, you must set some time aside every
day to write. You don't have to write. But during that time you
can't do anything else.*

No reading magazines, no filing your fingernails, no looking up favorite chapters from books, even if you think that task
will bring inspiration. No cleaning the bathroom sink or
scrubbing the floor. No telephone calling—especially not that.
Just sit there and . . . well, write. *You don't have to write. But
you can't do anything else.*

Just try it sometime. You find yourself going bonkers doing
nothing. You can't wait to get to the typewriter. Even with the
most modest literary ambitions, you want to push your pen
across the page or move the cursor along the computer screen.
No matter how inadequate you find your imagination, you're
forced to depend on it. You write. You listen to your inner
voice. You write anything. Maybe for a long time you sit and
study your cuticles and count the hairs on the back of your
hand, but eventually you write. You *have* to.

"That's what it must be like to pray," I realized as I began
my prayer journey. *This time is sacred. I might not have anything
to say to God, but I'm not allowed to speak to anybody else. No*

phone, no books, only the Bible. Pray. I don't have *to pray. But I can't do anything else.* There's an old paradox that goes, "Faith is a gift, but you *can* ask for it." During my prayer time I set myself to asking.

The other thing that helped me persist in my pilgrimage was an analogy made by my spiritual director relating to my marital life.

That winter, in the first year of our marriage, my wife rented a TV to watch the Winter Olympics. Every evening, instead of talking at dinner, we'd stare at skiing, skating, tobogganing, ski jumping. We'd watch the men's figure skating, the women's figure skating, the ice dancing. For four hours every night we watched TV. It was exciting, but after a few days I felt as though I were living with a stranger. We were both glued to the TV. During the commercials my wife and I conveyed some essential information, but we didn't talk long enough to communicate. We discussed the phone bill, the rent, and who was going to pick up macaroni and cheese at the corner grocery store or what to order from take-out Chinese for dinner, but we didn't connect. I didn't know what she was worried about, what she was dreaming about, what she cared about, and what made her angry. I had lost touch.

"We've got to talk," I finally said during one commercial.

"What do we have to say?" she wondered.

"We'll figure it out when we sit down to talk."

So we established the "half-hour rule," one we still abide by. According to that rule, we have to sit in each other's presence half an hour a day. No TV, no newspaper, no books. Maybe we don't think we have anything important to say. Perhaps the day doesn't seem very interesting. Perhaps our minds are empty of any witticisms. Tough. We sit and talk. And if we're there long enough, we discover that we have plenty to say. We hear each other. I find out about my wife's work and the article in the newspaper that irritated her and what her mother said on the phone that morning. She discovers that I have an irrational fear of the polar ice cap melting and an interest in the dollar's rise and fall on the international currency markets.

"Just as in marriage," my spiritual director told me, "you can take care of necessary business with quick petitions to God, but you're never going to get close and stay close unless you spend time together. You can't know God or even know what you want to say to him unless you commit yourself to praying. Not just here and there, or in passing. Set aside time every day to do it."

And if I did it every day, I just might find out who God was and who he was to me.

"Look back to your childhood. Look for times when you felt close to God. Look for what your past says about you spiritually," my guide had said to me. I didn't have to look far. There was something in my oldest memory, at least the oldest one that I can date.

I wasn't three years old yet. My mother was very pregnant with my little sister, who was born a few weeks before my third birthday. When the baby kicked inside the womb, I was encouraged to hold my ear up to my mother's tummy. It was like listening for the sound of the sea inside a conch shell or being told to look through the telescope for a view of a distant island when all you can see is your eyelash squashed against the lens. Although I could never really hear my sister kicking (or hear the sound of the sea in the shell), I could feel the warmth of my mother, and that was enough.

That day was a Sunday and my mother was wearing a pink seersucker maternity dress. I wore scratchy wool shorts and a white cotton shirt with stiff short sleeves that stuck straight out like a paper doll's. We stood together on a small riser in the church nursery, looking out the window at the older children playing in the sandbox and swinging on the swings. It must have been one of my first times at the church, because I was afraid to be left alone with the stout lady in the starchy dress that crinkled like tissue paper and the children who played on the swings. But Mom stayed with me, my hand in her warm hand. I felt comforted. I felt safe.

Did I know God? "We get our first glimpse of what God's love is like from our parents," I was told. We learn intuitively about God's nurturing from their nurturing. We come to understand how our wants are served and our needs satisfied. Our parents on earth as our Father in heaven. This concept worries me, because I wonder if those who had rotten parents will ever know a loving God (a God beyond the stern lawmaker and author of all natural disasters). But the concept also explains why this image of Mom and me has lingered with such clarity. It's not just chance that this is my oldest memory or that the setting is a church. There in the nursery I was comforted. I was safe.

In time that church we were visiting became our church, and its architecture became the scene for my earliest inquiries about God. The building wasn't your usual ecclesiastical Gothic but a variation on California Tudor, the half-timbered walls of a well-scrubbed Stratford-upon-Avon surrounded by day lilies, poppies, night-blooming jasmine, and roses that blossomed eleven months a year (one month to regenerate—a very limited dark night of the soul).

On Sunday mornings we were delivered to Sunday school rooms that wrapped around a sunny courtyard. Sometimes we were allowed into the sanctuary, sanctum sanctorum, where the arched beams in the ceiling disappeared into darkness like the ribbed beams of my father's boat sinking down into the keel. From the central beam in the apse a microphone hung from a black wire that seemed to come out of nowhere, dropping from the sky. And despite my father's best explanations, I believed it took our prayers up to heaven.

The minister was a kindly white-haired man who shared my first name, and when I was baptized I felt his wide hand encompass my small head, the drops of water messing up the cowlick that Mom had rigorously shellacked with spit and comb only minutes before. He looked holy to me, a central casting version of the divine. In Sunday school, we'd been told that no one knows what God looks like, but I knew the teachers were wrong. I knew exactly what God looked like. I had seen his picture on the cover of the record album of the Broadway show *My Fair Lady*. It was a Hirschfeld drawing of Eliza Doolittle as a marionette manipulated by Henry Higgins, whose strings were pulled by a bearded George Bernard Shaw from the heavens. God as playwright, God as puppeteer, God pulling all the strings. It was more convincing than the saccharine illustrations of Jesus I was shown.

I proved to be a champion Sunday schooler. I loved the songs: "Jesus Loves Me," "He's Got the Whole World in His Hands," "Joshua Fought the Battle of Jericho." I loved the art projects: making Judean homes out of sugar cubes, stick shepherds out of pipe cleaners, mangers out of Popsicle sticks. I loved the stories we dramatized, putting on old bathrobes and binding scraps of sheets on our heads with old stockings, marching around a stack of chairs until the walls of Jericho really came a-tumbling down. I was attracted to some of the teachings, especially Jesus' message of turning the other cheek. Here was a philosophy that transformed my older brother's nightly thrashings of me into a glorious martyrdom. My brother might have thought he was destroying me, wrestling me to the floor. But I was the true victor. After all, I had turned the other cheek.

In Sunday school we learned about prayer. We were taught how to close our eyes and bow our heads, telling the Lord what we wanted. "Don't worry about what you have to say," we were instructed. "It's just like talking to God."

I quickly decided, however, that it wasn't just plain talking. It wasn't like chatting with your stuffed animals or some imaginary friend. You used big words like *thou* and *thee* and *shouldst* and *wouldst*. You couldn't say just anything. If there was something you wanted from God or a favor you needed done, it was more like talking to an adult, one who wielded all the power. You had to phrase your request carefully, gauging your remarks with the utmost caution. You had to be careful. I knew about talking to adults. I had listened to them a lot. Parents, even when they think they're being harmless, can say hurtful things.

From an early age I was an eavesdropper. I discovered that if I lay on the living room floor with a few toys or a picture book, I could listen to Mom and her bridge-club ladies talk. I could collect valuable nuggets of gossip. Or at the beach, if I lingered by the grownups' towels, pretending to be absorbed in a sandcastle, I could gather information not available to my contemporaries. Sometimes my mother observed me and interrupted her friends, saying, "Little pitchers have big ears." But most of the time I went unnoticed. I had enormous powers of concentration. I was usually absentminded and had to be reminded countless times to do the things I was supposed to do, so how could my mother tell I was eavesdropping? How would a parent know I had overheard a remark when I rarely paid attention to what I was supposed to hear?

What I learned is that adults talked like parents when they spoke to kids, but they talked differently among themselves. They discussed with disarming frankness their offspring's shortcomings and received with gratitude the praise of their children's strengths. It was the praise I longed to hear—real praise, not just the flattery meant for my ears but a direct, un-patronizing, adult-to-adult compliment. (That it would be flat-tery for my parents never occurred to me.) "Such an unusual child." "He's very talented." "He paints very well for a boy his age." "Does he always sit there like that without saying a word, reading for hours?" "He has a lovely voice when he sings."

The sting came when I discovered adults laughing at me. I remember sitting on the bleachers at a college football game. Feigning fascination with the band's half-time show, I over-heard my mother's dear friend repeat a remark I had made earlier: "He said to me, 'Do you know that we four kids are born exactly two years apart?' Can you imagine that?" Then both women laughed, my mother just as hard as her friend. I felt betrayed. That my mother would think it funny too! Of course, I didn't understand that I had made a precocious com-ment about my parents' family planning to a friend who had twice as many children. I knew only that I was hurt.

The sting could also be administered by adults who weren't family or friends. I remember an incident that happened in second grade. At the time I loved to go to the dime store, where I'd spend hours walking up and down the aisles, studying every plastic ray gun, clipper ship, and antique car before I'd spend my five cents on a piece of candy or a stick of bubble gum. The aimless daydreaming was half the pleasure. I could imagine owning all the toys, or debating over which would be the perfect thing to buy if I had a dollar or two. Then one day, as I was gazing at a new model of an aircraft carrier, I overheard the woman who ran the store laughing at me with another customer. "He'll be here all afternoon and look at everything in the store before he buys something," she said. I felt cheated. Spied on. Found out. Deprived of my private delight. Quickly I bought my gum and walked out of that store, never to return again. I would deny myself pleasure rather than be laughed at. Pride goeth before a fall? My pride would rob me of delight.

The flip side of this was a painfully acute willingness to please and a hunger for a record of my success. The subtle, unintended effect of my early Sunday school experience was to learn that God liked us best when we took center stage and showed off. He expected us to be good in class, quick at raising our hands, prompt with the answers about God's love. We were adept at reciting any memorized Bible verses and confident in the solo we sang before a packed congregation at Sunday school graduation (where we were awarded certificates for perfect attendance). It was hard not to believe that God was interested only in goody two-shoes.

And yet what a place to shine! I loved my moments in the godly limelight. In particular I recall a church Christmas party at some member's house. All the other kids had retreated to another room for a round of Freeze Tag or Murder in the Dark. The sugar cookies with red and green icing had been eaten up and the pink punch in the crystal bowl was long gone, but I lingered with the adults at the piano as they sang all four verses of "We Three Kings" and grown-up carols like "Bring a Torch, Jeanette Isabella." I waited patiently for my opportunity.

"Rick, would you like to sing a solo?" the pianist finally obliged, answering my prayer. "Why not 'Silent Night'?"

Why not? I took my position in a corner of the carpet and sang in my clear boy soprano, the precise diction a result of imitating the English children in Mary Poppins. I was a little nervous, but not much. A hush came over the room. Everyone was listening to me. I hit the high notes without any problem. When I was finished, the applause came, the only clapping at the party, then the usual compliments: "What a nice voice! You sing so well. You should be on TV." I listened to the praise that came my way (and more important, the words that went to Mom and Dad); then I joined my own age group.

Later, in the car as we drove home, I asked my parents (disingenuously), "Did anyone like my singing?"

"Yes," they said, repeating what I had already heard. "They said you have a nice voice and you have perfect pitch." The words of praise were even sweeter the second time around. I could savor them in my mouth, as if licking divinity fudge off the sides of my teeth.

"Rick has a beautiful voice." Rick is rewarded. Rick is loved.

"Maybe I picked up some odd notions about what it means to talk to God," I told my spiritual director.

"We often do," he said noncommittally.

"I came from a praying family."

"Tell me about it."

Every night at dinner, as we gathered around our Danish modern teak table in the family room, my father served up a smorgasbord of prayer. "Let us reflect on the day," he said, and we bowed our heads. Beginning with the news he had heard on the car radio coming home from work and continuing with the latest family crises, he threw out morsels of concern for God and us to mull over.

"Hear our thoughts, Lord," he'd say, and we heard his thoughts. "Please be with Uncle Charlie as he recovers from his operation. We're thankful for the doctors who performed the surgery.

"Remember the people in the Midwest who are suffering from terrible tornadoes.

"We're thankful for the coming elections—that we live in a country where we have the freedom to elect our leaders. We ask for your wisdom to guide and help us as we go to the polls on Tuesday. May those who win honor you in their service.

(This was honest sentiment from a man who once told me it was a pleasure to pay taxes.)

"We were sorry to hear about the passing of Winston Churchill, but we trust that he's with you, and we're grateful for all the good things he did in his life."

And closer to home, he prayed for my sister to do well on a test the next day. Or he prayed for my brother to be able to finish his math homework before bedtime. Or he asked God not to make me too nervous on the night of my piano recital.

"It's the six o'clock news," one family friend said after hearing Dad's grace. "He keeps you up to date by mentioning everything he can think of."

He prayed us through the various space flights, the moon landing, the assassinations of Martin and Robert and John, the forest fires in the California foothills, the Vietnam War, and student protests. He prayed us through the deaths of beloved relatives and the births of distant cousins. He prayed us through Marilyn's overdose, the Nixon inauguration, the Watts riots, Watergate. He was encyclopedic in his approach. He included everything that came to his mind. It was his moment, his chance to address his Lord (and his captive dinner-table audience). With four talkative children, he wasn't likely to get another chance.

Sometimes he tantalized us with short references to the day's events, such as "We remember Cousin George," or "Thank you for the healing of Aunt Eleanor," or "Help the Haskin family." When we lifted our heads we had to ask, "What happened to Cousin George?" or "What was wrong with Aunt Eleanor?" or "Who are the Haskins?" Then for a few more moments the table was Dad's. He took the floor. He got to speak before mayhem resumed.

He had a fine theatrical instinct in his prayers. He used interruptions well. I was reminded of him once when I was at the opera and saw a diva respond with a shrug to a set that collapsed at the wrong moment. She gave it its due, the audience got rid of its embarrassed laughter, and then she went on with her aria. Instead of ignoring disruptions—which only would have drawn our attention to them—Dad incorporated them into his prayers. For instance, when my little sister and I started giggling, he asked God to bless our high spirits and good humor. When the German shepherd next door started to bark at some distant siren, he thanked God for the dog. And when our mutt responded, barking and leaping at the sliding-glass doors, Dad asked God to help us keep the pooch happy. When the telephone began to ring, as it always did for my older sister during her high school years, he thanked the good Lord for her popularity and requested a little more peace and quiet around the house. And when the timer went off in the kitchen, announcing that the rolls were ready to come out of the oven, he brought grace to a quick conclusion: "Bless us to thy service and this food to our use. And God bless the hands that hath prepared it." Then Mom would rush to the kitchen and rescue the rolls with her much-blessed hands.

What to do with interruptions in prayer? Include them, for goodness' sake. Maybe the interruptions are God's way of reminding us to add something or someone to our prayer list, the Holy Spirit once more clamoring for lordship over our time.

Dad's graces were a wonderful ritual, but when I think about them, they were holy in that nice way of church prayers. They were filled with graceful "thanks" and prayerful "pleases" and all-inclusive blessings. He would make the charming asides of a practiced preacher to elicit a laugh and be assured that we, his secondary audience, were still with him. But what about a praying person's aching request for love or popularity or attention? What about the kind of prayers I made in bed late at night, such as the wish not to have to sit alone at lunchtime at school, or the hope that if the teacher called on me in class I wouldn't get my words jumbled up, or the heartfelt request that would God please not let the class slugger hit the ball to me in left field? How did I know God heard those prayers too? Did Dad ever make them himself?

The odd thing about these corporate prayers is that they were a contrast to the violence of emotion I was discovering in the psalms. In third grade I memorized the hundredth and the twenty-third psalms. Before the congregation I recited "Make a joyful noise to the Lord" and the pastoral "The Lord is my shepherd" with my classmates, earning myself a copy of the Bible, a black embossed Revised Standard Version with colored maps of the Holy Land in back. But no one asked me to learn such passages from the psalms as "Break thou the arm of the wicked and evildoer," or "Break their teeth, O God, in their mouth," or "Let them be blotted out of the book of the living." Hadn't I wished that sort of harm on Lyle Donovan, who stepped on my sandcastles in nursery school, or on Brad Bruington, who pelted me with rotten persimmons one day when I was on my way home from school? Why didn't we memorize *those* passages? What would that have done for our spiritual education?

I knew intuitively about the dark, lurking terrors of life. Twice I'd had deep premonitions that seemed to be fulfilled— like the horrors promised by the biblical prophets. Once I woke up before the dawn, knowing that something bad was going to happen to my family. That morning my brother, Howard, broke his arm when he fell off his bicycle. Then one Good Friday when I was filled with a similar fear, I was almost relieved to learn that distant Alaska had been struck by the worst earthquake in years. As I stared out at the ocean, waiting for a tsunami to come, I almost wondered if my premonition had brought on the disaster. Were there no prayers big enough for such cosmic fears?

There's something else I find disturbing about my own prayers at this age. They were often phrased in a negative way. *God, don't make me have to catch that ball. God, don't make me have to eat this terrible casserole. God, don't let the house burn down while the baby-sitter is still here. God, don't let me be the last one chosen on the team.* Feckless, spineless, I lacked the courage of my convictions. It was as though I was afraid God would say no if I asked him for something really big and nearly impossible. I don't think I ever once had the gumption to pray, "God, make me a fabulous baseball player during P.E. today so that when the ball comes to me in left field I'll be able to throw it into home plate, making the runner out and turning me into the hero of the school."

I think I feared that if I asked for something big, my faith would be tested. I might stop believing in God—this little image of a weak, unterrible god. Safer to keep the petitions to a minimum. Safer to be less than anything I dreamed of. Safer not to have to risk being refused and rejected. Wasn't that my biggest fear? To ask God for something and then not get it?

As a child I knew only one confirmed atheist, my Aunt Gioia. My mother's older sister, she was a loud, opinionated, strong-willed woman with a machine-gun laugh and a chain smoker's mentholated breath. A single parent of four girls, she lived down the street from us, and our families assembled for every relative's birthday and every major holiday. At the dinner table she held forth, holding her beautifully manicured hands aloft like some Renaissance saint, the smoke from her cigarette rising as incense. But she didn't believe in God. And when we bowed our heads to listen to Dad's blessings, she kept her eyes open, staring blankly at the avocado Jell-O salad or the camellias around the birthday cake. (I noticed. I peeked.)

Why didn't she believe? The family story was told:

When Aunt Gioia was eight and her mother was expecting a child, she prayed and prayed for a little brother. She knew God would answer her prayers, for God answered all the prayers of fervent believers. Then came the big day and her mother went off to the hospital, but when her father came home, he announced that she'd been given a little sister instead—my mother. My aunt burst into tears. She wouldn't accept a sister. She went into her bedroom and slammed the door. When her mother came home from the hospital, Gioia locked all the doors and windows and wouldn't let the baby inside. Finally coaxed into reason, she unlocked the front door and held the newborn. In time she became a devoted sister to my mother, but she never forgave God and she never believed in him again.

Maybe that's what I feared. If I asked for something big, I'd end up like Aunt Gioia. Forever disappointed. I'd be like her at dinnertime: staring blankly at the avocado Jell-O salad during Dad's grace, or watching the smoke rise from her cigarette to a heaven she refused to recognize.

"You must have had some good influence, someone who set you on the right course."

"Like who?"

"A friend, a relative, a teacher. . . . What about Sunday school?"

There was one teacher among the horde of Sunday school teachers who brought me closer to God.

She taught a special Sunday school class that was held on Tuesday afternoons. I made a deal with my parents: if I went to the class on Tuesdays, I wouldn't have to go to Sunday school on Sundays. I could sit in church with Mom and Dad, or sing in the choir, or go see a (religious) movie with the older kids during worship. By then I was in fifth grade, and the teachers who taught regular Sunday school for my grade weren't to my liking. One was an ex-Marine with a buzz haircut and halitosis. His drill was the memorization of Bible verses and the unimaginative enforcement of a weekly Sunday school curriculum—notebooks, flannelgraph boards, puzzles, games, and dreary, moralistic stories. His partner was a dour woman who wore her hair in a French roll and had a streak of blue eyeshadow on her eyes. She didn't smile much, probably for fear of getting wrinkles. I didn't hesitate about what choice to make: I would attend Sunday school on Tuesdays with Mrs. Clarke.

It was a little embarrassing at first because of the unbalanced ratio of boys to girls—two or three to almost a dozen. After all, what self-respecting preadolescent male would want to learn about the Bible on a sunny afternoon when he could be catching pop flies at the sandlot? I didn't mind so much as long as there was at least one other boy. I didn't feel so queer. But if I was the only boy who showed up on a Tuesday afternoon, it was sheer torture.

(That's always been a problem with the expression of faith in our society. Men are afraid that it's women's stuff. That's one reason why men's prayer breakfasts and men's Bible studies and football ministries and baseball chapels exist. To take off the womanly taint stuck to prayer and faith. To make God look a little more macho. To make men feel maybe that it's all right and not downright loose-wristed to talk about Christ. It's also the sad reason that the newly ordained ranks of female clergy often face such an uphill battle. Men feel awkward enough talking about God, but it's a little easier if the preacher looks like Joe Montana or Frank Gifford.)

In fifth and sixth grades I stuck it out. I was one of three boys in the class (if we all showed up), and Dura Clarke was my teacher.

Mrs. Clarke was a Texan with jet-black hair, long bony fingers, paper-white skin, and dark eyes that were so deeply set you could barely see her eyelids. At times when the strain of keeping us under control became too great, she took off her glasses, put them down on her dog-eared Bible, and rubbed her deep sockets until I thought she would erase her eyes. "I think the Enemy is in our midst," she would say as we fidgeted at the table, someone lobbing a spit wad across the room. She was so sincere she caught our attention. "I want us all to bow our heads and ask God to restore us to our purpose."

Our main purpose was a glorious one. After juice and snacks, after hymn singing and Bible study, after making stained-glass windows out of colored tissue paper, we worked on making a movie. With her Super 8 camera Mrs. Clarke was filming the Bible, from the Creation to the Resurrection, soup to nuts. I came to this project fairly early. My first role was Abraham the patriarch, white cotton beard and blue robe over my corduroys and sneakers, footage of the Texas hill country spliced in later to represent the land of milk and honey. After practicing in the upstairs Sunday school room, we put on our costumes and went to the local park, where the key scenes were filmed. (I prayed no sandlot-playing classmate would see me in my biblical duds.)

The girls carried water vases on their heads and huddled around the pup tent that was Sarah's and my home. Sarah laughed her infectious giggle—the only humorous moment I could find in the Bible—when the angels without wings told her she would have a child. She was supposed to be even older than Dura Clarke, and at the time I thought that was ancient.

My great moment came with the sacrifice of Isaac. We actors walked to a fallen sycamore tree, the trunk white and gnarled. Isaac carried a bundle of kindling, and I had a kitchen knife hidden in my belt (we giggled when Mrs. Clarke called the belt a girdle). Mrs. Clarke shot a close-up of the knife, and then we walked to the tree trunk. Like any would-be Cecil B. DeMille, she gave her directions from behind the camera, for this was the era of silent home movies. "Tie him to the trunk, Abraham. Good, good. Raise your knife and raise your face. You're bewildered, but you know that you must follow God's will, so you obey. Good. Now you hear God's voice. He's telling you to stop. He won't make you take your son. You've passed the test. Look to the bushes. There you see a lamb— we'll splice it in later. You'll sacrifice the lamb instead. You're happy, overjoyed. You're a good servant of God."

I loved the acting. I relished playing Abraham's old age with arthritic fingers, stooped shoulders, and deeply furrowed brow. Like an old movie star in a silent film, I gave an exaggerated, histrionic expression of despair for Mrs. Clarke's rolling camera. My hand shook as I clutched the knife, and my eyes fluttered shut as I imagined the horror of it all. But when I heard the voice of God, a beatific, bewildered expression came over my face.

Later I played the aging Isaac, and then Jacob. Mrs. Clarke recognized my dramatic bent and encouraged it. Others carried water jugs on their heads or shepherds' crooks in their hands. I held a knife and spoke to God. More important, God spoke to me. That's what captivated me about these minidramas. God spoke. In the Bible people heard God's voice and obeyed it. God spoke to them in their tents, in fields where they were "keeping watch over their flock by night," on the rooftops of those Judean houses I had built out of sugar cubes. As I pondered this notion, I wondered if God would speak to me. Would he address me between dinner and my allotted half-hour of TV? Would he swoop down on our palm-lined block, where I flew a kite and rode my bike? Would he make an appearance in the school auditorium after we said the pledge of allegiance before an assembly? It was Dura Clarke's great gift as a teacher and the work of acting that made me feel that maybe I wasn't so far from Abraham, Isaac, and Jacob. God spoke to them. Why wouldn't he speak to me?

That became my fervent prayer. It wasn't an ultimatum. I never went so far as to say, "If you don't speak to me, I won't believe in you." But I did make my firm demand. I had become fixated on it. What did God's voice sound like? If you heard it, was it like hearing the principal's voice over the loud-speaker at school? Was it like the voice of the ghost in the TV show *The Ghost and Mrs. Muir* or the mother in *My Mother the Car*? Was it something that only you heard, making everyone else think you were out of your mind? Did God say actual words, or was the message just a feeling that came over you? (And if that was all, did it really count?) I even asked Mrs. Clarke one day after class, when the others had gone outside, "How do you know if God speaks to you?"

"My dear child," she said, looking at me with those dark, deep-set eyes that disappeared into her head and connected directly to her soul. She knew I was in earnest. She wouldn't laugh.

"You'll know," she said. "You'll know."

Then one early evening on a clear, rain-washed winter day, I was bicycling home from my piano lesson. The smog that usually shrouded the San Gabriel Mountains had lifted or blown out to the desert. I was coming to a hill behind my school with an incline good for coasting around the corner and all the way to the next street. You could lift your feet off the pedals and sail on the wind. It was getting dark, and the mountains were crushed grape at the bottom and gold at the top. The royal palms bent with the breeze as I lifted my feet off the pedals. And in that moment God spoke to me.

He was in the mountains, in the sunlight, in the dead palm branches clapping against the trunk. He was behind the schoolyard's chain-link fence and above the lone Frisbee thrown into the air across the newly sodded field, the sweet smell of grass tickling my nose. He was in the street lamps that just that moment clicked on—or did I only notice them just then? He was in the Clementi sonatina that had just left my fingers and the smiley face and three stars it had earned from my piano teacher. He was in the meatloaf dinner that would be waiting at home and the Wednesday night elation of having got through more than half the week without any mishaps. He was in the approaching twilight and the fading pink. He was in the wind, the night, the day; he was in me. I knew God spoke to me, words no more profound and no less than the great "I am" echoing through the words of the prophets and the psalms. As I careened down the hill, borne by gravity and some strange emotion I had never known before, I cried because I knew God was.

It would be wrong of me to suggest that was the only transcendent moment in a childhood that had its share.

There were the times we watched *Peter Pan* on TV, the taped version of the Broadway play with Mary Martin in it. It was broadcast every spring in my childhood. I remember going over to my grandparents' house to watch it on a color TV with all my cousins, lying on a bearskin rug with my head on the dead bear's stuffed head as I watched Mary Martin fly, held aloft by an invisible wire like the one attached to the microphone in church. I remember when Tinkerbell drank the poison. The glass went empty and her light flickered, gradually going dim. Just then Peter flew in, discovering his dying comrade. The poison was meant for him, yet "Tink" (sacrificial soul) drank it to save him. At that magical moment Peter— Mary Martin in tights—turned to the camera and begged everyone in the TV audience to clap. "If you believe in fairies, clap," he (she) said. "If you want Tinkerbell to live, you have to show that you believe. Clap, clap, everyone clap!"

Back then I clapped. Everyone clapped. Even my brother, who when told that elbows on the dinner table squished the fairies usually pounded on the table hard with his elbows. But when he heard about Tink's demise, he clapped. And I clapped harder. I believed, and I wanted to show that I believed.

I was drawn to things that required faith. Willingly I suspended my disbelief. It was easy to appeal to my imagination. Some things appealed so readily to my fears that I dreaded them. They called up monsters in the twilight and made me shudder. The flying monkeys in *The Wizard of Oz*, the rumbling chords of "A Night on Bald Mountain," the kettledrums in "Peter and the Wolf." Monster movies were out of the question.

I was the ultimate sucker for TV appeals. I had to watch hours of Jerry Lewis's Labor Day weekend telethon for muscular dystrophy. When my brother insisted on changing the channel, I burst into tears. "But Howard," I tried to explain to him, "as long as we keep the TV on, the little boy in the wheelchair will live. But once we turn it off, it's all over. The TV *has* to stay on for him to live." Like Tinkerbell's flickering light going dim. Clap, clap. I believed. Clap, clap.

And then there were the great space-age milestones of our era, some bringing fear, some lending thrills. I learned early to dread the sound of the sonic booms that rattled our plate-glass windows and made me fear that the Russians really were coming this time. But how could anyone forget the magic of being carried outside in his pajamas on a summer evening and having his father point to the heavens at a moving star that was our first satellite flying overhead? I remember my father's excitement and the nighttime sky better than any speck of light.

When I was six, my mother took me to my first professional play, a bus-and-truck production of *The Sound of Music* at the old Biltmore Theater downtown, not far from the red neon sign near Pershing Square that declared, "Jesus Saves." It was the last show to play in the old theater before the place was torn down and turned into a parking lot. We sat in the top row of the upper balcony beneath a few frescoed *putti*. "The bloody-nose section," an older man sitting next to us observed. (It was years before I realized he was making a joke about the high altitude of our seats.)

The curtain rose. The Alps looked like cardboard, even from our distant vantage point. The Trapp family house was obviously made of fabric; a wall rippled when an actor slammed a fake door. One backdrop came down from the fly-space and almost bounced off the stage floor. My eye wasn't fooled. But I was transported by the music. The combination of orchestra in the pit and real people singing on stage moved me. I found it intoxicating that people could make music out of what they had to say and what they felt as the plot progressed from song to song. I was hooked on musical theater.

From then on, the years of my childhood could be marked by whatever musical I saw: a *Showboat* revival, Meredith Willson's *Here's Love*, *Brigadoon* in the round, a high school production of *Carousel* that left me sobbing, *Mame*, *Man of LaMancha*, *You're a Good Man, Charlie Brown*. I asked for tickets for my birthday; I bought all the records and spent hours in the music store, fingering the sheet music. A biography of Richard Rodgers was my favorite book at the library. The imprimatur "Original Broadway Cast" became for me what *nihil obstat* is to an orthodox Catholic reader. I turned on the record player, and if no one was looking I danced to the music on our family-room rug.

Soon every other word of conversation was a cue for a song in my head—not only the hummable refrains but the obscure introductions and multiple verses. I discovered the power of a song to transform my moods, always for the better. The heartbreaking songs—the likes of "From This Day On," "You'll

Never Walk Alone," and "Somewhere"—had cathartic powers. I could be smarting from the familial injustices that came of having an older brother twice my strength, and still I could talk myself into well-being by rattling off the patter of a song like "Wouldn't It Be Loverly?" from *My Fair Lady*. The meaning of the words was unimportant. The rhythm and tune satisfied.

"He who sings prays twice," said a sign in Gothic script posted in our choir room at church. For a long time I stared at that during rehearsals and wondered what it meant. Then I understood it a little bit. When you sing a song, it stays with you; it sticks in your craw and repeats forever in your mind until you get a new song to get rid of it. It's like praying without ceasing. Throughout the day you do a thousand other things—you brush your teeth, solve a math problem, do your homework, run a cross-country race—but all the while you've been singing of the sublime beauty of "Dulcinea." Even when I wasn't sure I believed, I found phrases of hymns and religious songs repeating in my mind.

"O, clap your hands all ye people, sing unto God with the voice of triumph." It becomes impossible to separate a biblical text from a tune once you've learned to sing it. I read "If with all your heart ye truly seek me, ye shall ever surely find me" and hear Mendelssohn, or read "This is the record of John" and think Gibbons. "O Clap your hands with a voice of triumph" is Vaughan Williams. How can anyone hear the phrase "And he shall reign forever and ever" without humming Handel? You sing the words before they make any sense, like a child warbling "Round yon virgin, mother and child." The sense of it comes much later. You believe, clap, clap. You clap. You believe.

The most popular moment of each Sunday school session came at the very end of class when a green light went off next to the clock at the front. That was the signal that the adults were finished worshiping. We were free. We could grab our mimeographed sheets of Bible verses and our clay crèches and our tissue-paper stained-glass windows and race down the stairs to meet our parents. But what I loved even more, the signal I looked for, was the sound that came a few seconds before the light went on.

The ushers pushed open the side doors of church on the last verse of the final hymn (modulated up a half-step), and the lovely, thrilling roar of hundreds of people singing like all the Whos in Dr. Seuss's Whoville shook the casement windows and the branches of the magnolia trees. Clap, clap, they believed.

Because I knew how to sing, I knew how to praise God. I knew it inside of myself. I knew that bubble-up-inside-you feeling. I knew how in only a few bars you could go from minor to major, from sorrow to joy, from adagio to vivace. I knew how people sang from the stage, as though their lives depended on what they could put into music.

Praise him with the sound of the trumpet:
    praise him with the psaltery and harp.
Praise him with the timbrel and dance:
    praise him with stringed instruments and organs.
Praise him upon the loud cymbals:
    praise him upon the high sounding cymbals.
Let every thing that hath breath praise the Lord.

"But you still don't know how to ask," my spiritual director said. He had become impatient with me and my ramblings about my past, as though my faith had been frozen at some preadolescent level without any of childhood's natural trust. This was a hurdle I dreaded facing.

"Ask?" I wondered.

"Ask for what you want. You don't trust that God will give it to you."

He quoted Scripture at me: *Therefore I say unto you, What things soever ye desire, when ye pray, believe that ye receive them and ye shall have them.*

Verily, verily, I say unto you, Whatsoever ye shall ask the Father in my name, he will give it you.

"That doesn't seem fair," I said, sounding very much like a child objecting to the arbitrary nature of parental rule. "The onus is on the person praying. As though if you don't believe hard enough in what you're asking, you won't get it. That doesn't seem fair."

"How will you know if you don't ask?"

Ask? I shuddered at the memory of people on religious television shows asking God for houses, for cars, for vacations in Hawaii; of people begging for first prize in the Publishers

Clearing House Sweepstakes. It's as though God were the ultimate home-shopping companion. Order anything you like and then give him a few numbers from your moral stockpile of goodness and devotion. Offer up your niceness as collateral. Charge it on your good-values credit card. I remembered the weird experience of going to a scientific, nonchurch church in Hollywood. A friend had asked me to go with her. She had said she found the place helpful.

I was led into a large, windowless room, like the meeting hall of a secret society. The walls were painted a surgical green, the floor covered with beige wall-to-wall carpeting. Organ music came from speakers hidden above the ceiling's acoustical tiles. We sat in folding chairs while the "minister" (who called himself a "doctor") led us in a "treatment." We closed our eyes and visualized what we wanted.

"You want a cabin in the mountains?" the preacher/doctor said. "See it; picture it; make it come true. Believe it." He looked for a situation appealing to the Hollywood congregation. "You want to be a star on a television series? Imagine it. Imagine the audition, the things you say, the people you meet. Picture yourself on the set with the actors you want to work with. Or you want to fly first class? See the experience in your mind's eye. See that wide, soft first-class seat. See the stewardess serving you complimentary champagne. Hear the beautiful classical music playing on the headphones. If you believe in it and ask for it, you can have it."

I squirmed uncomfortably. The treatment struck me as sacrilege. Who was going to give us all these good things we were asking for? Was just picturing them what it took to have them?

Would a well-directed, fertile imagination suddenly bring us the starring role or the first-class seat? It was nonsense. The nonfrocked minister in the beige linen suit seemed a charlatan and his treatments a sham. But now my own spiritual director, a tweed-suited, clerical-collared divinity school graduate, seemed to be suggesting that I do the same thing.

"It's so materialistic to ask God for things," I complained.

"Well, aren't some of your needs materialistic?"

"Yes, but . . ." I looked for more objections.

"Don't you think God cares about what you eat, where you live, how you work?"

"Yes, but why should he bother listening to me? Doesn't he have much better things to do with his time?"

"You know that old gospel hymn, don't you? 'His Eye Is on the Sparrow.'" He hummed a bit. "That says it all. 'He watches over me.'"

"Well, if he watches over me so carefully, he knows what I want already. I shouldn't have to tell him. I shouldn't have to ask him. He should have it all figured out."

"Maybe," my spiritual director said, while eyeing the light that illuminated on his phone, "just maybe he wants to hear it from you. Maybe he wants to hear you say it yourself. Maybe he knows you need to say it. When you need a raise at work, you ask your boss for it. Like your boss, God needs to know you care."

I wasn't so sure. When I left the parsonage and made my way through the dusty park to the subway, I thought again of the Bible record. *Whatsoever you ask the Father in my name, he will give it you.* I hated asking anyone for anything, let alone my

Father in heaven. As a kid, I hated to ask my own mother and father for things. Not that they weren't generous; not that there were strings attached. It's just that I could always think of good reasons why I shouldn't be given a new book or couldn't go to the movies or wouldn't be able to take acting classes in summer school. The more I wanted something, the worse it was. I didn't want them to know how badly I wanted something. I wanted to please. My imagination worked overtime so I wouldn't have to ask for things.

I can recall something that happened when we visited New York City for the first time. It was 1965, the year of the World's Fair, when so many kids I knew made the pilgrimage to New York. We didn't go to Flushing Meadows to see the fair because, as my father (California chauvinist to the core) explained, "We have Disneyland back home." Instead, we traipsed the city streets for twenty-four hours. I loved it—loved the dust, the noise, the bustle, the popcorny stench, the sweltering July heat. It even rained that night, a summertime novelty for a Southern Californian. We climbed the Statue of Liberty, took the elevator to the top of the Empire State Building, walked through Times Square, where through the windows of a darkened bar I spied go-go girls dancing. We threw coins in the fountain at Rockefeller Center, held our ears in a hurtling subway, ate breakfast in the basement of the Seagram's Building, inspected the Impressionist paintings at the Metropolitan Museum of Art, and hurled paper airplanes out of the window of our skyscraper hotel, watching them float out of sight.

But as we were walking the streets on the morning we left, I got a bad case of the hiccups. We passed a streetside vendor with a large cart and an umbrella. I hiccuped vigorously, and he held up a small carton of orange juice. Did I want some?

Standing on a corner of Fifth Avenue with my family, I was suddenly struck with indecision. What *did* I want? Would orange juice help?

"You can have some," my dad said. I looked at the short, white-haired vendor holding out the juice. It would mean a sale for him, money in his pocket. He looked sympathetic. Except that drinking orange juice didn't usually work to get rid of hiccups. Suddenly it embarrassed me that we were stopped on a New York sidewalk because of me, and I wanted to get moving.

"What do you want?" teachers asked when you raised your hand in class.

"What do you want?" parents asked if you interrupted their telephone conversation. "What do you want?" they wondered when you woke them up in the middle of the night because you had had a bad dream or felt sick or scared.

What did I want? I didn't know, and at that moment on that street corner I was frozen with indecision. Stymied by an excess of self-consciousness, caught in confusion, I wondered whom I should try to please: my mom and dad (what did they want?), the man selling juice, or me?

The memory of the moment startled me. At the time, my indecision won. It was easier to say no. I shook my head no at the vendor and shrugged off Mom and Dad's concern, hiccuping repeatedly as we crossed the street and continued down the sidewalk to one last New York landmark, a blast of air-conditioned cold attacking us whenever we passed an open door.

Indecision won then as it often did later in my life when I struggled over career choices, life choices, spiritual choices. Sometimes I was like a person who buries a "to do" list deep in papers on a desk, hoping that the onerous tasks would somehow be done when the missing note was unearthed months later. I would rather that someone else do the asking for me, or that the decision be made by proxy. Maybe it was because I spent so much time wondering what the answer would be—second-guessing the response—that I talked myself out of decisiveness. I was the last person I knew to ever ask a boss for a raise or a promotion. Did I do that with God? Did I spend so much time trying to figure out what he was like and what he wanted that I gave up being honest about what I wanted?

Just maybe he wants to hear from you. Tell him. Be direct. Believe that he wants what you want. *Just ask.*

"But I've done that before," I told my spiritual director. There was a time when I boldly asked, believing that God would give me just what I wanted.

O God, I'm still stuck at this level. I hate to ask for things. What if you refuse me? What if you say no? My faith wavers constantly. "This must be what the Lord wants," *I think. But can I ask for it? No. I'm afraid. Even now. Afraid of being rejected.*

With the onset of puberty I flirted dangerously with not believing in God at all. Maybe it was hormonal. Maybe it was intellectual. Whatever the reason, religion for me was an on-again, off-again thing during adolescence. At one moment I was the star of our church youth group, leading the congregation in contemporary worship services, hoping to shock the oldsters with a rendition of "One Tin Soldier" that was meant to be a rabble-rousing call to peace, passing out daisies as we sang. At another moment—in fact, at almost the same moment—I was sharing lustful asides with my best friend in the choir stalls about the girl in the front row who wore a backless Hawaiian print dress.

At a time when I wanted desperately to believe, I went with great enthusiasm to a youth Bible study at a church that was more evangelical than ours. One evening I sat on a leather sofa next to a gas-fueled fake-log fire in the fellowship hall of that church and listened to the leader outline what it meant to believe in Jesus. I hoped to give my heart to Jesus too, but I felt something phony and manipulative in the guitar music and songs, and when one of my cohorts found some charismatic spirit that flung her to the tiled floor in holy ecstasy, I wanted to laugh, not sigh. (Secretly I wished she were wearing a backless dress.)

When I was back at my usual church, our youth group went to see the movie *Woodstock* and then held a weekly Bible study on the book of Galatians. "Stand fast therefore in the liberty wherewith Christ hath made us free . . . ," Paul wrote, and our minister emphasized that this book of the Bible was about freedom, but all I could think of were those hippies in the Woodstock movie who (high on music and hallucinogens) had taken off their clothes in the rain and were dancing naked in the mud. Free? Is that what real freedom was?

In the church basement our youth minister led a sex education class, and for several weeks I sat with a group of fifteen- and sixteen-year-olds as we gingerly discussed our feelings for the opposite sex. At one point the psychologist leading the session made some passing reference to masturbation. "What's that?" one fifteen-year-old asked. The room fell into a stunned silence. I don't know what embarrassed me more—the clinical explanation the psychologist gave or the mind-boggling possibility that one of my contemporaries didn't know what masturbation was.

Lust is a confusing thing. Sex seems a sure way to heaven. It's so close. The forgetfulness, being lost to yourself in someone else's arms. The drive for passion . . . what a lovely servant, what a dangerous god. Not until I was married could I ever come close to acknowledging the power it had over me. Not until then, God, could I see Eros as one of your gifts.

After that I wandered away from church. By the time I was a junior and senior in high school I had decided it wasn't cool to believe in God, and when I started college I figured it would be much more convenient to call myself an atheist.

As an atheist I wouldn't have to answer any awkward questions about who I was or what I believed. I could indulge in some modest hedonism without any qualms. I wouldn't have to go to chapel on Sundays, wouldn't have to defend any unpopular positions, wouldn't have to think about Saint Paul when I wanted to think about sex. I could be cool, hip, existential (whatever that meant). I was traveling all the way across country for an Ivy League education, and I figured my Christianity was excess baggage—like my California flip-flops and hang-ten T-shirts. It could go.

I arrived eagerly on the campus, finding walls covered with ivy (as advertised), long-haired classmates full of radical notions about impeaching the president, the dormitory lounge filled with late-night *I Love Lucy* fans ready to challenge orthodox notions about faith as quickly as they changed the TV channel. But what else should I discover? That my roommate, the valedictorian at his Pittsburgh high school, a straight-A student, and a brilliant physics major, was literally a card-carrying Christian. He kept three-by-five cards with him at night when he read the Bible. On them he wrote down passages he found inspiring and passages that would help him when he was arguing theology with any of the doubters in the dining hall. His Christian friends from campus often met in our room for group Bible study, and the quotes were marshaled out after the strumming of guitars and the singing of folk songs that I'd thought I'd left behind in California.

It was God's little joke, no doubt. You can't run away from the Almighty. He's the hound of heaven. *Whither shall I go from thy spirit or whither shall I flee from thy presence? . . . If I take the wings of the morning and dwell in the uttermost parts of the sea; even there shall thy hand lead me, and thy right hand shall hold me.* God knew I was faking my unbelief. No matter how far I went, he would be there. In fact, he would be in my own room, looking out for me.

I held on to my atheistic position for several months, until finals loomed and I started to feel desperate about my standing in my Princeton class. In that dark winter of my first reading period—darker and colder that year because of the oil crisis and the efforts by all to turn down the thermostat and to turn off the lights—I worried that too many late nights in the lounge trying to solve the problems in the Middle East in heated discussions had taken their toll. While my roommate had gone to bed punctually at 10:30 every night, I had reveled in the freedom of a dormitory without parents and with few parietals. I had slept late a few too many mornings, missing classes. I hadn't studied hard enough. Now that I had to face finals, I didn't know how I would manage without help.

One January afternoon I wandered into Princeton's monumental chapel. The bright midwinter sun pierced the multicolored windows and bathed the pews with bright patterns—an effect like autumn leaves on a forest floor. No energy crisis here. I seated myself in the back. Someone was practicing Bach on the organ up in front, the reeds and trumpets echoing off the gray stone walls, rattling plaques that memorialized the war dead.

I didn't kneel. I didn't open a prayer book or Bible. I simply closed my eyes and said silently, *Lord, I need help.* I spoke as directly as I had when, at one of our church's annual youth services while I was in high school, I had led the congregation in prayer with the self-conscious opener "Hi, God." Now, however, I wasn't trying to shock my elders or shake anyone out of a comfortable, complacent pew.

Hi, God. I need help. I need to pass my finals.

So there it was. I had asked God. I wanted something. I needed it from him. And I wasn't greedy. I didn't expect an A or a B on my finals. A C would do—what was wryly called a "gentleman's C" back then. I just wanted to pass Shakespeare and French 202 and the artfully named Physics for Poets.

Having asked God for help, I clearly believed there was a God to speak to. I wasn't just addressing the stained-glass windows or the bronze plaques or the wood carvings of apostles on the choir stalls. I hadn't even bothered to reintroduce myself. It didn't occur to me that I needed to. My behavior puts the lie to that old standby that "God helps those who help themselves." On the contrary, God is there for people who can't figure out how to help themselves.

Did I believe he really would help me? I must have. That's what desperation can do. It's the reason poor, bewildered inner-city dwellers often know more about the Lord than rich and well-insured suburbanites with blue-chip portfolios. The poor have to trust. They have to believe. So do the poor in spirit—like me. Back then I believed that any two camels could push themselves through the eye of a needle if God could help me squeeze out a passing grade.

"You were a foxhole Christian," my spiritual director observed.

"I was in a foxhole," I agreed.

"You needed help, so you prayed to God. That's the most basic aspect of prayer."

"But I still wonder . . . wouldn't God have helped me anyway? Did I really have to *ask* to be helped?"

"I refer you to a story in the Bible—one of the parables of Jesus. You should remember it—the parable of the importunate widow."

This is really one of the oddest parables of all. It opens with this preamble (as sobering as the surgeon general's warning on a pack of cigarettes): "And he spake a parable unto them to this end, that men ought always to pray, and not to faint."

The story goes, as Jesus tells it, that there was a certain widow who kept applying to a judge again and again, asking for justice against her opponent, until the judge, weary from her repeated visits, finally gave in. The point is this: Would God not do better than the unjust judge? "And shall not God avenge his own elect, which cry day and night unto him?"

Where did that put me? Where was I meant to be? Clearly in the role of the pestering, importunate widow, badgering the judge until he gives in. The thought irritated me. Okay, so God is more merciful than any corrupt judge, but does that mean he tacitly approves of pestering? Day and night. Without ceasing. And if God knows what's in our hearts anyway, why should we ask? Why go to all that effort over and over, again and again? I had rather hoped God could be more direct. Ask and it shall be done. Your word, master. But no. Who was master here? God seemed to delight in my importunity, my servanthood.

"Asking is an important part of believing," my spiritual director said—and he was so wise here, so helpful. "Maybe God likes us to be repetitive in our requests. It's an exercise we need to go through. It's his way of preparing us for what he wants to give freely.

"Look again at another passage I've mentioned to you before: 'Therefore I tell you, whatever you ask in prayer, believe that you receive it and you will.' Believe. That's hard for a skeptic like you."

Once again he had read me clearly. When I asked, it was with the full knowledge of God's refusal. It was as though I had secretly supplied the Almighty an out. "Dear Lord, give me a job that I'll find fulfilling," I prayed, while muttering under my breath, "It's really a lot more than you can do. It's more than anyone can do. You don't realize how rough it is out there. When did you ever look for a job? It's a dog-eat-dog, swim-with-the-sharks world. I need to look out for number one. I'm afraid you can't help."

My sophisticated self worked overtime telling God what he couldn't do. Did I believe? Well, no.

So ask, ask, ask. Be importunate. Be insistent. Do something about what you're asking. Is it possible that you can become so tired of wishing that God would make something come true that you'll start believing it yourself?

"He wants us to be importunate because it helps us," my spiritual director said. "It helps us believe. 'Believe that you receive it and you will.'"

"I'll try."

He broke off a piece of toast. "By the way, did you pass all your finals that year?"

"Yes. I worked hard. I crammed. I stayed up late. I went to the library. I dropped by the chapel. I was willing to do anything, even believe in God, to pass."

"Did you believe he would help you?"

"I must have."

"Why?"

"It was finals, my freshman year. He wouldn't have wanted to see me flunk out. Everybody would have been disappointed."

"Good." He put his long fingertips together, gracefully forming a Gothic arch with his hands. "Do you believe he'll answer any of your prayers now?"

I shrugged. "I don't know."

"Do you remember what it says in the Bible about Jesus in Galilee after he'd been preaching to the people for a while and performing miracles? Suddenly he stopped. His work came to a standstill. No more healing. No more preaching to the people. The Bible has this telling phrase to explain it: 'And he did not do many mighty works there because of their unbelief.'"

After my first freshman finals, God and I were at a standoff. I was willing to acknowledge his existence, showing him the greatest tolerance, like a teenage girl including her little brother on a date (with a guy she probably doesn't like much anyway). I was ready to believe God existed. I was not so ready to believe in his powers.

When finals came around again, I was a little more confident of my own ability. That can happen in the aftermath of an answered prayer. If your faith isn't strong, if you're still too proud to be thankful, you can easily convince yourself that you succeeded by your own merits. Or you can convince yourself that your knowing all the right stuff for the test was a mere coincidence. You start thinking that you would have done fine anyway. No need for divine help. Nice to have, but not necessary. An added frill.

I wasn't willing to make God a part of my daily life at Princeton, but during those four years I discovered him in other places. Outside of chapel, outside of the Bible study I visited once and hurriedly left (Christian folk songs ringing in my ears). Closed out of Sunday mornings, God crept into my weekdays. He made unexpected appearances on the syllabus.

I was an English major. And I had professors—intellectual, well-respected, recognized authorities in their field—who actually mentioned the Bible in the classroom. They had a way of smiling when they did it, enjoying the irony that Chaucer, Spenser, Milton, and Donne would have better luck at getting us to turn to the Scriptures than any well-meaning preacher or pamphleteer. "Of course, you know," a professor would say, drawing us in with his flattering air of familiarity, "what Chaucer is referring to is the biblical passage in Genesis when God promises that he will never, ever punish man with an all-destructive flood again."

We nodded our heads. Our professors appealed to us where we were weakest, the academic's Achilles' heel: intellectual snobbery. No one dared admit that he or she hadn't opened a Bible since distant Sunday school days—but when our professors talked, we nodded. We understood. Of course, we knew.

The subtle and unsubtle references to Christianity in many of my English classes, especially when it came to anything written before the nineteenth century, had a cumulative effect on me. I decided it was all right for some people to believe. It was okay to ask the difficult faith questions. I saw that Christianity could come in palatable doses of good taste, which was even more appealing to my aesthetic snobbery. It could inspire the most profound literature, music, art. Bach cantatas weren't only formal experiments in music theory; they were also fervent expressions of faith. George Herbert wasn't just writing pretty poems; he was writing about something essential to his whole being. Flannery O'Connor's dark tales were comprehensible only when you applied to them her deep-seated Catholicism.

Forgive me, God, I'm still an intellectual snob. It would be un-derstandable, perhaps, if I had a first-class mind. I don't. I have a B-plus mind. I was never in the top ten percent in my high school, never scored in the top bracket on my college boards. When I ap-plied to Princeton, I was told my chances weren't very good. "A weak possible," the admissions office said. I'm still overcompensat-ing for that premature appraisal, still trying to prove I'm worthy.

At this age I made an unusual choice for my senior thesis. I decided to write on the Victorian man of letters John Ruskin. At the time I explained it by saying I was interested in Ruskin's love of art and Italy, but now, upon reflection, I think I was also attracted to the dilemma of a man who was trying to reconcile his strict Calvinistic faith with his visceral attraction to the visual arts. He failed in the end, miserably—as anyone must fail who tries to make a direct correlation between good faith and good taste. It can't be done. The most sublime art can come from the most dreadful people, and the loveliest of modern saints can be satisfied with the most saccharine, cast-plaster statues and painted-velvet scenes. "God is not always choosy about the vessels of his grace," the writer Robertson Davies once said, and it's true, from overweight opera divas to debauched painters. Arresting beauty doesn't necessarily re-flect religious truth, but I appreciated Ruskin's stubborn ef-forts to prove it did because I wanted someone to prove it for me, to codify in some reasonable way the connection between faith and art.

As I wavered in my faith, I wavered in my belief in myself. I was half confident and cocky and half scared to death. I couldn't figure out why. I liked to believe that God was a crutch only for the weak. I liked to think I could do very well on my own, thank you very much. And then huge doubts would assail me.

It was a time in my life when people said nice things to me about my talents and congratulated me on my achievements, and I couldn't believe a word they said. They're flattering me, I thought. I had an inferiority and superiority complex all in one.

As a natural charmer, I knew how easy it was to put someone on your side by a gracious word of praise. How was I to believe that my flatterers weren't as insincere as I was? I dismissed kind words as the balm of snake-oil salesmen. It takes one to know one.

One night at dinner, at the wide refectory table draped in linen beneath the flickering candles in the silver candelabra at my college eating club, I sat next to a psychology major who was attacking a fiercely individualistic, highly intelligent biology major from India. "You cling to your faith because it's comfortable," said the psychology major. "You go to church and believe in God because it's the way you were raised. It's a mindless habit."

"On the contrary," the Indian fellow said, "I was born and raised a Hindu."

The comment rattled me. I identified with the psychology major, the learned skeptic, the independent thinker. And yet, who proved to be going against the grain? Who was the unique one? Who had taken the road less traveled? For the moment I wished I were more like the Indian fellow. He believed in something. Every Sunday morning he got up early to teach Sunday school, wearing his blue blazer with the crest of some old school in India. While pursuing a rigorous scientific field, he had still chosen to assert his faith. The unshaven, jeans-wearing skeptic barely rolled out of bed in time for Sunday brunch.

Another one who shattered my preconceived notions was the university chaplain, a fervent, Christ-believing World War II hero who had somewhat outlived his campus welcome. With a rich Scottish accent and a high Presbyterian style (the concept seemed an oxymoron), he delivered withering jeremiads Sunday after Sunday on the college's worldly ways. From my vantage point in the choir, I could listen to him remind us of the work of the devil, singling out the exclusionary practices of the eating club where I belonged. I could smile at his histrionics, honing my own imitation of his preaching, "It's satanic! It's demonic! It's wrong, wrong, wrong, wrong!" But I admired his independence. I liked his commitment. I loved him for being unpopular. Nothing mealymouthed about him, nothing lukewarm. He wore Christianity with style. He even showed a sense of humor when I congratulated him on a sermon one Monday morning. "Well, at least you weren't asleep!" he said with the thick burr that had gotten only thicker the longer he'd lived away from Scotland.

If I were to become a Christian, I thought then, I would want to become a Christian like him. I would wish to be outrageous, anachronistic, a tightrope-walker. But I was a fence-sitter, and fence-sitters can stay stuck for a long time. It's amazing how long such indecision can last, even when you're searching, looking, reading, praying, sometimes landing right in the lap of God, then retreating back to your post on the sidelines out of the way. What did I believe? I didn't believe much in God. And I didn't believe much in myself.

"Have you ever heard of negative prayer?" my spiritual director asked me.

"Negative prayer?" It seemed a contradiction in terms. After all, wasn't prayer by its very definition an affirmation? When you prayed, you told God, "I want," "I desire," or "I need." The very act of praying seemed to be a means of saying, "I am," "I think," or "I believe." And all those usual sign-offs were affirmations: "Amen," "Let it be so," "Selah." How could prayer be a negative?

"Sometimes what we say to ourselves, what we think we want so badly, is destructive—even if we don't say it outright to God."

"But as a prayer?"

"Yes, prayer can also be negative. Look at the biblical evidence," he said. And then he began to pull biblical examples out of the air like a magician pulling rabbits out of a hat. He referred to the incident in Acts (I had to look it up) when Paul comes across a sorcerer, "a false prophet," who was trying to turn the new converts away from their belief. Paul, filled with the Holy Spirit, zaps the man and makes him blind—"only for a season" (which must have been a kind afterthought for the overzealous Paul). That was a sort of negative prayer.

"Remember how Jesus takes offense at a fig tree that bears no fruit?" he asked. This one I remembered. Jesus was walking along the road with the disciples and saw a fig tree with nothing but leaves on it. He cursed the tree and it withered before their eyes, as in a scene from one of those nature films of blooming flowers now suddenly run in reverse.

"Or there's the time when Jesus casts out the demons from a man and throws them into a herd of pigs. Do you remember what happens to the pigs?" Sure I did. The possessed pigs charged off a cliff in an act of mass suicide worthy of a modern apocalyptic cult. Maybe this was meant as a joke for kosher-keeping Jews, but I've always wondered if the owner of the pigs got recompense for Jesus' miracle. The healing was a positive act, but what of the fate of the pigs?

"There's tremendous power in a negative wish," my spiritual director went on. "If you repeat it over and over to yourself, it can become a prayer. All the kind, good, positive things you hope for can be obliterated by those negative, self-destructive thoughts. Think about it. If the Holy Spirit could be used by Paul to blind someone, or Jesus could wither a fig tree with a simple curse, what damage can we inflict on ourselves by our withering, crippling thoughts?"

Sermon finished, point made.

Then, in his usual distracted manner, he looked at his watch and opened the sliding mahogany doors of his study. The sunlight poured in, illuminating a shaft of dust raised on the old Oriental rug as I walked past. He fumbled at the series of locks on his front door, rang for the elevator, and bid me good-bye, giving me a hug, leaving me to think. How impatient I became with him, but I think there was a genius to his ways. He made me do the mental footwork. I had to connect the dots.

Negative prayer. Back in college we used phrases such as "He hosed himself," "He shot himself in the foot," or "He flushed himself" when a person did himself in. I suppose that was a kind of negative prayer at work.

In college I was in a small, tight-knit, all-male singing group. Twice a year we'd audition new members. In a campus lounge we'd listen to singers try to sight-read a few bars of close harmony and sing a couple phrases from the national anthem. Most guys were pretty good, but once in a while we'd hear a fellow who was so shy, so uncertain, so lacking in confidence that we knew before he opened his mouth that he would fail. Maybe he could sing, maybe he had a nice voice, but you could never tell from the way he handled himself. It was torture to listen to his intervals and watch him blush as he warbled through a few measures of "Oh, say, can you see" while backing up to the corner of the Steinway. You wondered why he put himself through it. You could see the poor fellow thinking, "I'm not very good at this. I can sing in the shower, but not here. I can't even carry a tune. What in heaven's name inspired me to sign up for this audition anyway? I can't take it anymore. I've got to get out of here. Help!"

Finally the misery would be over—misery as great for us as it was for the would-be singer. And after the door was closed and the singer out of earshot, we shook our heads and repeated the obvious: "He flushed himself. He hosed himself. Did himself in."

You could tell the moment the auditioner came into the room how he thought he would do. His attitude became a self-fulfilling prophecy. The losers looked like losers. I remember seeing some of those guys around campus later. They weren't losers elsewhere. They walked with confidence in the campus dining hall, swaggered as they carried their trays, certain that they had friends waiting for them. Or they were quick thinkers in seminars, leaning back in their chairs, listening to the discussion warily before contributing an incisive observation, making a clever connection no one else had made. But when they were out of their realm, even before they sang, their bodies shook.

I knew how they felt. When I was out of my element, I acted the same way. As a kid playing baseball or football or soccer, I always went where the ball was least likely to go. And when I came up to bat, I repeated this mantra: "I'm never going to hit this. I'm never going to hit this. I'm never going to hit this." I never did.

By the time I went to college I had learned how to protect myself. I had gathered a whole arsenal to save myself from the inner voices that wished for my failure, to guard myself against futile collapses of my fragile confidence. Believing that a man is what he thinks about all day, I found ways to make my thoughts as complicated as possible. Sophisticated, I thought. Witty, cynical, self-deprecating. But where do you draw the line between self-deprecation and self-hatred?

Don't get your hopes up too high. This was one of my self-protective devices. I think it's a common parental warning, because parents are afraid to see their children disappointed.

They prepare the child for disappointment even before it comes. "Don't be overconfident about making the team," they warn. "After all, you're younger than the other kids and you don't have as much experience. Don't get your hopes up too high." Or they say, "I'm glad to see that you're trying out for the lead in the senior class play, but there's a lot of competition and it's a very hard part. Don't get your hopes up too high. I don't want to see you disappointed."

A wise child soon learns the message. You repeat it to yourself, turning it into a magical incantation. You decide that if you don't wish for a thing to happen, then you won't be let down. If you don't want something too much, you'll be happy with whatever comes. Pessimism masquerades as pragmatism. "If I don't hope this will happen, if I don't expect it, then maybe things will turn out all right. I'll be pleasantly surprised."

What a contrast this is to the faith, the optimism, even the blind belief of those who were healed by Jesus! Take the woman with "an issue of blood," who believed that she needed only to touch the hem of Jesus' garment to be healed. Or take the centurion, who believed that he needed only to have Jesus say the word and his ailing servant would be healed. Jesus didn't even need to go to the centurion's home; Christ's distant healing would be enough for the faithful soldier. *According to your faith be it done to you.* That's all anyone needed—a little faith.

I distrusted faith like that because it seemed to stem from ignorance. Blind faith, like blind confidence. Cocky people, I told myself, acted that way because they didn't know any better. They weren't sensitive enough to perceive their own faults. They couldn't be stymied by doubts because they didn't have any doubts. And yet what good did my religious doubts and self-doubts do for me?

As I walked away from my spiritual director's place and headed for the subway, I lingered over his words. *There's tremendous power in a negative wish. It can become a prayer.* I recalled auditions and interviews where I had disqualified myself quickly. While working as an actor, I had once told a prospective agent, "I'm not really a very good actor. I haven't had enough experience." Disarming candor? Hardly. I had hosed myself, flushed myself; I had done myself in. The agent must have wondered what I was doing in her office. She must have wondered how I had talked myself through the door.

I remembered doing an audition for a Shakespearean troupe, reciting Prince Hal's speech from *Henry IV,* part 1: "I know you all, and will a while uphold / The unyok'd humor of your idleness:/ Yet herein will I imitate the sun. . . . " I identified with Hal. I liked to think that so far all I had done was a mere prelude to who I would become. *Herein will I imitate the sun.* Staring out from the stage at the empty red-velvet seats, I believed my glorious dawn wasn't far away. So I shouldn't have been surprised when the director said to me, "That was very nice."

Immediately I had my doubts. Quickly I explained that I didn't know how to do Shakespeare, had never been in a Shakespearean production, hadn't really studied him much.

"I liked what you did," the director reiterated. "You have a nice lyrical quality."

Amazed that I hadn't been asked to leave yet, astounded that I had repeated the entire monologue without being interrupted, stunned by the man's appreciative comments, I rambled on, digging myself a deeper hole. "I don't think I really have the voice for Shakespeare. My voice is too high. It would be nicer to be a baritone. And I've never done any stage combat."

The director became irritated. Almost red in the face, he insisted, "I liked it. You did a nice job."

I backed off the stage like a lowly servant retreating from a throne room. Outside I felt sick. Why didn't I believe in myself? Why couldn't I accept a simple compliment with grace and courtesy?

Cynically I decided it was because I never gave an honest compliment. I was a manipulator. I used flattery to make people like me. It was my stock in trade, a verbal tic. Usually there was an element of truth to what I said, but truth-telling wasn't my real purpose. Compliments were a way to please people, to make people enjoy me. So why would I believe anything nice that was said to me?

Several years later, when I was no longer acting for a living, I thought of the new job I was starting. Riding the subway to the office, jammed in the rush-hour train, I recalled the negative prayers I must have said as I began other new jobs. Not "Lord, let me succeed," but "Lord, don't let me be a miserable failure so that I attract attention." *Don't let me catch this ball. Don't let it even come my way.* It was one of those minor miracles of human stamina and stubbornness that I had succeeded at anything. So I was a good faker. But why fake out God?

And then it came to me, the point the good minister was driving at: you can't lie in a prayer. You can't fool God. He doesn't hear just the words; he knows the real wish of the heart. *Out of the abundance of the heart, the mouth speaks* (Matt. 12:34). God had heard the prayers of my heart, no matter what words had come out of my mouth.

I thought of all the prayers I had written in my journal, prayers God had been kind enough not to answer: "God, make me a famous, sexy soap-opera star." "God, make me a Wagnerian tenor." "Lord, make me the author of a runaway best-seller that makes so much money I'll never have to work hard at anything again." "Jesus, give me a better body than the one I've got." (A few trips to the gym could have helped.) "Christ, why can't I dance like Fred Astaire?" (The countless dance classes I'd taken should have answered that question.) Had I really believed any of my prayers? What had been the prayers of my heart? Did I really want to succeed?

As I was traveling uptown to take on a writing assignment for a magazine, I wondered if I was doing what God wanted me to do. That was the help I wanted from my spiritual director. That was why I had gone to him in the first place. I wanted to know my vocation. I wanted to settle an issue that had plagued me for years. And now he was asking me if it wasn't my own limited faith at fault. Was that the advice I needed to hear? Was this the word meant for me?

I was right where I'd been ever since I graduated from college. I was still struggling with the same issue.

"Perhaps, until one starts at the age of seventy to live on borrowed time," Graham Greene writes in his autobiography, "no year will seem again quite so ominous as the one when formal education ends and the moment arrives to find employment and bear personal responsibility for the whole future." Graduating from college, I concurred.

I wasn't ready to leave a world where everything was planned for me and enter one where I had to take responsibility for myself. What would I do? Where would I go? How would I live? I dreamed I could do a thousand different things, from running a Fortune 500 company to becoming a monk, and yet I didn't believe I was capable of anything.

At the time, I wished for a pair of parents who thought very little of what I did. Then I could prove myself or defy their wishes. But my parents' only declared wish was for me to be happy. Their all-embracing, all-forgiving, unconditional love embarrassed me, partly because it seemed so undiscriminating. I wanted to be told to enter the family business—if there was such a thing. I wanted to be ordered to do something patently practical, like writing advertising copy or giving piano lessons or selling encyclopedias door to door. I hated to be told I was smart, clever, talented, and capable of deciding for myself what to do. I hated to be given the chance to pursue whatever I chanced to dream.

The height of my misery came on graduation day. After wearing my cap and gown and receiving my sheepskin, I came back to my dorm room to do some final packing. Tears tumbled down my cheeks as I put old textbooks in boxes, rolled up old posters, folded blankets, and packed pillows in a steamer trunk to be sent ahead to California. In my self-dramatizing way, I was sure life was coming to an end. I would never discuss the fate of the modern novel again, never harmonize at midnight under a neo-Gothic arch, never swim in a fountain, never dance in a moonlit courtyard beneath blooming wisteria, never have so many friends in one place again.

Everyone else on campus seemed to be moving toward a promising future. But all my summer plans had fallen through. I'd lost a job, messed up a relationship, given up a summer sublet. I wouldn't be going to New York City, where half my class planned to converge. Instead, I was headed home. With my diploma shoved into a manila envelope, I would be driving across the United States with Mom and Dad. The only plan I had for my future was to paint the outside of my sister's house.

That hot summer, as we drove along the interstate, the plains had never looked so flat or the desert so desolate, the Joshua trees like prophets foretelling my despair. "The pathetic fallacy," my mentor Mr. Ruskin would have called it. My emotional state determined how I saw the landscape. When Mom and Dad and I came over the Cajon Pass into the hazy Los Angeles Basin, I felt I was staring at the quintessential paradise lost. The orange groves were shrouded by June smog, the vineyards were being squeezed out by flimsy housing developments. Gray palm trees nodded their heads behind dusty billboards. Ribbons of concrete freeway cut through the hills. I breathed in the stench of diesel exhaust, and the familiar sight of Forest Lawn with its phony statue of David with a fig leaf struck me as a tragic blight on the mountainside.

I wanted to turn back; I didn't want to go home. That night, as I lay in a bed I had long outgrown, my feet sticking out at the bottom, I felt like a scared child. With only the slightest effort, I could imagine I was a mental patient recently released from an institution with no prospects for remedial job training. There was no future. This was the end of the line.

All through my growing up my father had a set of practiced phrases he used to shore me up. Before hanging up from a long-distance telephone call, he always signed off, "Love ya." Backstage after a high school performance, or when I was handing him an award-winning essay, or when I was catching my breath after a cross-country race, he always exclaimed, "Your mother and I are proud of you!" When I was discouraged or disheartened, he proclaimed, "I'm sure you'll do the right thing." Now I had to hear those phrases continually at short range, and they didn't make me feel good; indeed, they made me feel worse. I didn't feel worthy of my father's pride. I wasn't so sure I'd do the right thing.

As I painted the white stucco of my sister's house with painstaking slowness, taking ten times as long as a professional painter, I stared at emptiness, the white paint spreading over the sun-drenched white walls. A whole day would pass without my speaking to anyone or hearing anything but the radio. The wind rustled the bougainvillea; flies buzzed in and out of open windows; the neighbor's dog barked; the phone rang once or twice. The biggest challenge of my day came at lunchtime, when I had to decide whether to pick up some Mexican food from a nearby taco stand or drive to McDonald's for a burger. Lying in the grass for my lunchbreak, peeling patches of latex paint off my fingers as I listened to the fruity-voiced announcer on the classical radio station make foreign musicians' names sound even more foreign, I found I could be very happy doing nothing. Emptiness—the blank canvas, the clean tablet, the empty mind, the white wall—was a very good place to start.

"Schedule a daily time for prayer," my spiritual adviser would later say. "Put it on the agenda." "Schedule a time for nothingness," he might as well have said.

That summer of my twenty-second year, when I had decided my life was over, I found the healing power of nothingness. To my surprise, I enjoyed going nowhere, having no ambition, just painting white on white. It was as though my own palette needed to be rid of its muddied colors, as though my brushes had never been cleaned between dabs of fuchsia and burnt sienna. I was in too much of a hurry. I needed to slow down. I needed to catch up and consider all the colors I'd splashed on the ground and spilled on my smock. For a change I needed a new canvas—pure, empty, flat white to take the new clean colors. No, I didn't pray while I was painting. I didn't even meditate. But maybe the experience helped me years later when I did pray.

I could visualize the pure white, the emptiness, and then the dripping rollers adding some cream on top, filling up the crevices of the stucco in a graceful pattern with no predetermined plan. I recalled how Dad, when I couldn't sleep at night as a kid, would come into my bedroom and massage my back, telling me, "Relax. Make your mind blank. You can see nothing but a blank wall. And behind it another blank wall. And behind that another blank wall. The white is soft, smooth, comforting. Your eyes are heavy. Your arms and legs are heavy. You feel yourself floating. You can think of nothing. You can see nothing but the blank, empty wall."

I still do that. I still meditate using those images. The blank wall, emptiness, nothingness. Nothing but God.

The summer days had no order to them. I painted when I wanted and stopped when I felt like it. My only vague deadline was sometime in September, when my sister would give birth to a baby and the mostly empty house would suddenly be filled with a family. September was the month when I needed to be moving on, to attach myself to some life goal. September was *always* when things started up again. It was a time to go to back-to-school sales and to buy fresh notebooks from the stationery store, to take up piano lessons again after the summer's hiatus. It was a time of soccer practice, school dances, football games, the new fall season of TV sitcoms. In September I'd give up nothingness for good.

I thought of the baccalaureate service back in the Princeton chapel the day before graduation. Trying to keep my own personal confusion at bay, I listened to one of America's great spiritual leaders give his speech to the assembled senior class and their parents. I sat in the choir, where we had sung the Randall Thompson "Alleluia," as inoffensive a piece of music as you could find for a nondenominational service: the only words were "alleluia" repeated over and over again. But the speaker himself had no compunction about being spiritually specific. He used biblical language and stressed the Christian concept of charity. Afterward I remember one parent complaining that his advice had been too parochial, that it was meaningless to those who didn't adhere to Christianity. Perhaps it was, but it inspired in me a goal for my life.

"I would like to be happy," I announced to a classmate after the service, as though I'd just discovered the secret for decoding Mayan hieroglyphics. No one is ever supposed to be changed by those long-winded springtime exhortations; no one is expected to follow their advice. Maybe I didn't, but meditating on the theme inspired a certain direction in me. After all, as Kurt Vonnegut once said, we don't go to church to hear a sermon but simply to daydream about God.

"I would like to be happy," I repeated to myself, holding on for dear life to the remote possibility.

So I daydreamed about being happy. To be happy—what did that mean? I began to define it almost in negatives. Happiness meant I wouldn't do the practical things urged on graduates by well-meaning advisers in the college placement office. I wouldn't listen when they shook their heads in those recession days and said, "Don't come to us ten months from now looking for a job. By then it will be too late." (Too late for what? I wondered.) Perhaps I was trying to affirm that the lucrative offers of New York City bank training programs wouldn't make me happy, nor would the Washington, D.C., internships. Even then the quandary of a classmate who claimed, "I'm trying to decide between twenty thousand dollars a year at Union Carbide and going to Union Seminary," struck me as faintly ludicrous. If you were spelling it out in dollar terms, you were probably going to take the money.

Happiness had to be something inside of me, not someone else's decision about what I should be. I wouldn't be rich or powerful or blindly ambitious. I would be happy. Maybe that doesn't sound like a noble decision—"to be happy," as though I were trying to stave off the near-certain misery I saw in most of my other options. But clinging to that thought kept me focused as I stared at my sister's stucco walls. Somehow, somewhere, I would be happy.

As the latex paint wrinkled in the sun, I hatched a plan. I would go to Florence, Italy. I would be a writer there, living a gloriously Bohemian life, eating only pasta and beans, having long, leisurely conversations with other expatriates about the quality of life, reading Dante and Ariosto in the original, owning nothing more than the clothes on my back. The money I earned from this endless painting job would get me there. When I found picturesque garret accommodations, I would survive by becoming an English teacher to wealthy contessas and nouveau riche industrialists (supplementing the meager earnings of pen). Surrounded by great art, I would soak up the sun, the language, the music, the refined aesthetic sensibility.

It was an outrageous dream, one I needed the boring hours of painting to indulge. I'm surprised no one laughed (did they even smirk?) when I shared it. "That sounds like a good idea," my ever-tolerant parents said. "To discover your vocation means following your dreams one step at a time," a wise older friend suggested. "Going to Italy sounds like the perfect next step."

Outrageous as it was, much of that dream came true. I arrived in Florence in October when the city was bathed in a diaphanous light that hung on the gray cypresses, reflected off the golden palazzos, spattered the rust-colored vineyards, and shone on the silver olive trees climbing the hills. Within a week I found a job teaching English. I found a viewless room to rent and volumes of Dante and Ariosto to read (with a well-thumbed Italian-English dictionary in hand). Within two weeks I went on a weekend excursion to the monastery in Vallombrosa, where the golden leaves had fallen just as they do in a simile from Milton ("Thick as autumnal leaves that strow the brooks in Vallombrosa"). There I met some expatriates who readily indulged my desire for long, leisurely conversation on the declining quality of life back in the States. We decided that no one else read the great books anymore. No one talked using the fine language we did. No one ate fine, elaborate meals. No one lived the good life as we did.

Lord, I still smell the fragrance of Italy in my dreams. The smell of rosemary cooked over an open fire, the scent of coffee sprinkled with cinnamon in the morning, the lovely crunch of the first basil of spring. I see the flowers: the geraniums falling from balcony grills, the purple iris multiplying under olive trees. I sing them a song as I pass that tells of the wonders of May when you're young and in love with life.

I could, if you like, paint a rich, vivid picture of the two romantic years I spent in Italy: the long dinner parties in lofty, dank apartments; the restaurant scenes with pasta, Chianti, and thin slices of veal; the palazzo I moved into, where in lieu of rent I walked an Italo-American contessa's overfed dachshund and practiced Italian with her aging retainer. I could describe the students of English who footed the bill for my two-year Florentine sojourn. I could introduce you to the soigné ladies in my afternoon class who made me blush with their flirtatious charm. You can imagine picnics, if you like, in the soft Tuscan countryside, and a rarefied aesthetic life of concerts, operas, plays, films, and rambles through the city's overstocked museums. A surfeit of riches, a dazzling array of choices, a once-in-a-lifetime opportunity. You could probably imagine a picture of me—I have a copy—looking long-haired and effete, staring out across the Arno River with the Ponte Vecchio behind me, bearing the weight of declining Western Civilization on my furrowed brow.

I sang too. Opera, lieder, art songs. I had a short Italian voice coach who greeted me at his palazzo in a black beret as he unlocked a row of double bolts on the front door. His wife had been a diva in the forties, and the apartment was filled with her portraits: Butterfly, Violetta, Mimi. "Sing to the pictures," he said. I sang with all my heart, believing that Italy was heaven on earth. "If you have a heart and a shirt, sell the shirt and move to Italy," went an old proverb. I agreed.

And yet, to be frank, the reality of those years was something different. I remember spending long hours chasing after orange buses, rushing unprepared to classes I was supposed to teach, going to music lessons and voice lessons and dance lessons, hurrying to the little American church where I was the most loyal of choristers. I went twice to the Uffizi in two years, visited the real David at the Accademia only once. I was too busy preparing American high schoolers for college entrance exams, tutoring a German-American in spelling and a Dutch boy in math, trying to earn enough money to pay for my rent (after the dog-walking stint)—and for the dinners, the concerts, the operas, and the music lessons.

How impatient I was with the American tourists who clogged up the streets of the town, drinking in its beauty, slowing me down on my busy errands and appointments. I remember running into one otherworldly California acquaintance who proposed that we linger over a cappuccino at some bar. "Can't," I said with irritation. "Too busy. I've been up since five-thirty. I had to take the six o'clock bus to teach a group of Italian NATO officers at the War College. I taught housewives at two, college students at three. I've got to practice the piano for a lesson tomorrow, and I have two classes to teach tonight. I don't have time to relax."

I didn't write the Great American Novel when I was in Italy. I didn't even keep a diary most of the time. My greatest literary effort was poured into entertaining letters home. Was I happy? Most of the time I was worried about wasting my time. I was worried about not doing anything significant with my life. Stuck in a European backwater, I was going nowhere. I had no real definable purpose in life, no future. What was my goal? I tried to shrug off these worries as unnecessary appendages in my grand evolution—like adenoids that could be excised. But the anxiety was there. In this sunny, good-natured Catholic clime, I was full of Calvinistic guilt for enjoying myself. So I became busy, looking for a purpose in my busyness.

"Feigning frenzy," a friend used to call it. Rushing here, rushing there, too hurried to look up at the golden light on the watermelon-shaped Duomo, too impatient to enjoy the long, leisurely conversations I insisted on having.

When I left Florence for the last time, my Italian friends gathered at the train station, waving white handkerchiefs with good-natured Florentine self-irony. *Ciao, bello. Ciao, Rick. Addio.* As the train moved down the platform around a corner and they disappeared out of sight, I knew that one chapter of my life had come to an end. My two-year *Wanderjahr* was over. Now I would do something serious. But what?

"You're so dismissive of your Italian experience."

"I don't mean to be. It was great. It was the first time I went off and did something on my own. I made the agenda. I found my own apartment, own friends, own jobs. I went to a city where I didn't know a soul and discovered I could do all right. The experience gave me self-confidence."

"Good. I'm glad to hear that."

"But I guess I'm confused by it because it didn't have anything to do with moving me forward in any sort of career."

"Are you so sure?"

"It was an interlude," I said. "A slight break in the ordinary. A vacation, a retreat."

"Don't you believe God uses such experiences to show us the direction we're meant to be going?"

In Florence, one point in my compass had been the American Church, a curiously out-of-place northern neo-Gothic structure in a southern Renaissance town. Where every other church was cavernous and grand, here was something quaint and twee. Built at the turn of the century, it had tan brick walls, fake travertine marble arches, a wheezing Victorian organ, and walls of brass plaques memorializing the donors. It was as though the American expatriates, incapable of making their mark on the old stones of Florence, had shipped over a suburban confection to wear their graffiti.

After I arrived in Italy, the rector was one of the first people I looked up. In my search for work and a place to live, he proved helpful. Out of more than just gratitude I promised I would come back to worship the next Sunday. The church was Episcopal, and the service proved more liturgical than any I had experienced—almost as foreign as the one in the Duomo. I stumbled from program to prayer book to hymnal, trying to follow the American rite, but something about the theatricality of it appealed to me. I returned. In time I used the basement for practicing my singing and the choir loft for showing off. I came to attend services regularly, convincing myself that the choir-singing was good for a musician like me. If anyone asked me why I went—particularly my left-leaning anticlerical Italian friends—I apologetically explained that it was "for the social life." Indeed, I counted many of the other churchgoing expatriates as friends, and I was relieved to be in a place that celebrated great American holidays such as Thanksgiving and Halloween. I lingered at coffee hours to chat with academics and art historians on sabbatical. But saying I was there to meet people was a white lie. I was also there because I was looking for something spiritual.

I found words in that hallowed space, words about God. They particularly stood out in this worship context because everywhere else Italian words were being spoken. Coming from the crowded streets and buses where I struggled to eavesdrop on Italian, I stepped into a world of bold, Elizabethan, majestic *Book of Common Prayer* words. They seemed both familiar and strange. We presented ourselves "to be a reasonable, holy, and living sacrifice." Why "reasonable"? "We have followed too much the devices and desires of our own hearts." What were those mysterious devices? That word made me think of Machiavelli. And then there was this very sweeping statement: "We are not worthy so much as to gather up the crumbs from under thy table"—a phrase that I quickly associated with Italian *trattorie* and dried crumbs of tasteless Tuscan bread on the white linen tablecloths.

At every service we sang or chanted psalms. When I was feeling self-conscious, I couldn't decide where to put the emphasis in singing about, say, going down into the pit and being rescued from my adversaries and saved from my transgressions. At an Easter Eve service the pastor asked me to sing the longest psalm imaginable—one about "fire and hail, snow and fog" and "wild beasts and all cattle, creeping things and winged birds." I chanted for an eternity, trying desperately not to lose my pitch or my place as I squinted at bars of music in the dimly lit sanctuary. I must have gone on for fifteen minutes, with incense billowing and candles flickering. "Praise God for all these things indeed," I thought, wondering what my Puritan forefathers would have made of this mock popery. "Praise God if I can finish this list."

But oh, there was something tantalizing about the cumulative effect of those liturgical words week after week. I could never concentrate on them all at once; it was too much, like a heavy diet of creamed sauces and red meat. Only one or two passages would stick in my mind, and then often because of some odd association—the way one turns "for which it stands"

into "for witches' stands." My thoughts wandered during worship, but I liked hearing those words. Part of me couldn't believe they were repeated year after year in the same manner. I
wanted to ask the impertinent schoolboy's question, "But
what does this have to do with me in the twentieth century?"
Another part of me, a deeper part, found comfort in the mere
ritual. I would stop asking "Why?" or "Who?" and let the time-
less words wash over me like the light streaming down from
the stained-glass windows. It was a pleasant feeling that stayed
with me, like the faint aroma of incense that stuck to my tweed
jacket for days after Easter Eve.

Among the people I met at the American Church was a
Harvard history professor on sabbatical, the sort of woman
who intimidated me in my college days. Smart, articulate, and
not one to suffer fools gladly. In ultrachic Florence, where
women took pains with their fashionable (and presumably uncomfortable) footwear, she looked startlingly out of place with
her sensible "earth shoes" and no-nonsense corduroys. But
she had a wry way of smiling when she talked that I liked,
whether she was describing the impossible-to-follow political
conflicts of Renaissance Florence or her local fruit and veg-
etable man. At a church coffee hour in the rector's study, as I
nibbled on my Styrofoam cup, she said something that I was
to ponder over for many months. "Whenever anyone asked
Jesus a question or tried to stump him, he would simply tell
them a story. Pin him down, and he tells you a story."

Stories I could deal with. Indeed, the stories of Jesus appealed to me. They were unlikely, unexpected. There was the
parable of the talents: the lowly servant who carefully pre-

served the one coin he was given was scorned in favor of the lordly servant who took his five coins and doubled them with investments. Caution wasn't rewarded; good fortune came to the servant who took a risk. I liked the parable of the lost sheep: the one lost lamb was worth as much as the whole flock. The message of the brides seemed a striking contrast to the usual browbeaten Christian humility: "Is a candle brought to be put under a bushel or under a bed and not to be set on a candlestick?" The story of the good Samaritan seemed a little obvious, and it easily became confused in my mind with the name of a dozen hospitals, but the parable of the prodigal son was good enough to be irritating. How would you feel if you were the older son? After you've done everything right (probably feeling self-righteous in the bargain), your black sheep of a brother suddenly comes home, having squandered his inheritance, and is not only welcomed with open arms but given the fatted calf you were counting on eating yourself? Who would set *this* up as a paradigm for behavior? What sort of justice is it? Only a first-rate storyteller would try it on his audience. Only someone who wanted to shake up the play-it-by-the-rules caution of nature's unprodigal sons.

Influenced by the parables, I debated my choices for the future. "I won't be overly cautious. I'll try something different, squander my inheritance perhaps—chance a risky investment of my talents." My mom and dad came to visit me in Italy that spring. After they had been in Florence for several days, I told them with some trepidation that I was trying to decide what I would do with the rest of my life. We were walking down one of Florence's narrow streets, only wide enough for us to proceed single file. Without direct eye contact it was easier to talk, as it is when you're riding in a car. I told them that I had been offered a job as a high school teacher at a fancy Swiss boarding school—a bird in the hand, really. And then I wondered aloud whether I should maybe pursue my singing, ". . . or do something different like that."

As Dad followed me down the narrow, lightless alley, I waited for his response, his benediction.

"I don't know," he said in that agonizing way he had of turning over important decisions to his own children. "You should do what you want to do. Take a risk. Do what you enjoy." *I don't know*, he'd said. Never ordering, never forcing, never commanding, trusting me to be able to make my own wise plan. As I walked ahead of him, sidestepping a parked motorcycle, I knew what I would have to do.

"You should give your father more credit," my spiritual director said to me.

"You think so?" What son ever gives his father enough credit?

"Yes. He guided you. He was enlightening you spiritually. He wanted you to follow the dreams you had. To do what you wanted."

"Well, you should see what I did next."

"Why not become a teacher instead?" my old friend Patti said to me. "Why an actor?"

For two years she had lived the life of a New York actress, waiting on tables, hustling for interviews and auditions, making the rounds from agent's office to ratty rented rehearsal rooms in the Ansonia Hotel to pay phones (where she checked on her answering service with the roll of dimes she kept on hand). She had impressive printed cards with her name and picture on them, and she'd explored the exercise classes, dance classes, voice classes, movement classes, and acting classes that keep actors and actresses busy at their craft in the long fallow periods "between jobs." She knew the New York rental-housing market and where to look for a reasonable sublet. She knew how much to pay for a room in a shabby apartment building filled with actors roving from summer stock to regional repertory to waiting on tables while hoping for a commercial that might air on the networks nationwide. She knew what I should do to be a New York actor, and she wasn't encouraging.

"Teaching seems a lot saner," she said.

"It doesn't make a good story," I explained. "Consider the schoolteacher who wishes he were an actor and inflicts on his

students dramatic readings of Shakespeare with him in a starring role. The teacher with pear-shaped tones who uses the
classroom to prove he could have been Olivier's successor." I'd
seen enough of frustrated ambition and thwarted creativity. I
didn't want to be the kind of person who exclaims, "If there'd
been a bit more money, I would have been fabulous on the
stage."

"Compare that," I said, "with the talented actor and singer
who later gives up a promising career on the stage for the love
of teaching. That makes a better story."

"A much better story," she agreed.

So went the discussions I had in Patti's large Upper West
Side apartment. I couldn't quite explain to her what an impres-
sion the prodigal son had made on me. Not that I would de-
scend to the prodigal son's level of riotous living, filling my
belly with the husks meant for swine. I just wanted to do what
seemed unexpected. I wanted to shake things up. To myself I
looked starchy, straitlaced, stiff, and conventional. I could have
been one of the subway riders in a sacklike Brooks Brothers
suit reading the *Wall Street Journal* folded vertically. Instead, I
bought the actor's uniform: black pants and white shirt for
busing tables, sweats for exercise and dance classes, and a lot
of denim for in between. With the help of friends like Patti I
had a résumé put together, exaggerating what few stage credits
I had earned, and I had my picture taken—two glossies: one of
me with a stiff, insincere-looking smile and the other with a
blank, empty-headed expression that I hoped was very sexy.

My first job was in a summer stock production of *South
Pacific*. The theater's locale, a Victorian dance pavilion on the

edge of a lake in upstate New York, was idyllic. All summer long we watched the corn rise, the apples ripen, the day lilies bloom and die. At night we listened for approaching thunderstorms coming out of the hills, waiting for them to interrupt the theatrical proceedings with hailstones on the dance pavilion's tin roof.

With vigor I threw myself into the enthusiastic "Let's put on a play" atmosphere of the company. I hammered nails in the sets, glued costumes together, coaxed props out of theater patrons. I sang in fund-raisers at the town's old folks' home and was part of a Rodgers and Hammerstein Fourth of July festival on the village green. I was interviewed by the local paper and entertained by the local citizenry. Backstage I shared in the opening-night jitters, hugs, and kisses. But on stage, in my romantic tenor role as Princeton-educated Lieutenant Cable from the Main Line, PA, I felt like a sham. I knew I could sing all the notes—my high G I was particularly proud of—but I didn't know a thing about acting, and from the awkward way I walked through my part, it must have been obvious to the last row in the bleachers. Even at the curtain call, when the applause was generous, I could only smile woodenly at the appreciation.

You see, I didn't "feel" my part; I wasn't "in touch with my emotions"; I hadn't "found" my character; I hadn't explored his motivation; I didn't know where his vulnerabilities lay. Back in New York I had enrolled in a Greenwich Village acting class that met in the basement of a doctor's office, and when each class began we had to do exercises based on different emotions: anger, rage, love, jealousy, hostility, hate, despair, fear, joy, anguish, terror. Our teacher would call out the different emotions as we writhed on the indoor-outdoor carpeting (until the nurses from the doctor's office upstairs complained). When our teacher called out, "Anger!" "Rage!" many of my classmates dissolved into shrieking tears, while like the character from *A Chorus Line* I felt nothing. I had no emotions. I believed I was an emotional midget. Now on stage at the Victorian dance pavilion they'd found me out.

In the afternoons before performances I tried to do some of the exercises I had learned in acting class. I stood many furrows out in the cornfield and acted to the budding ears of corn. "Tell us, Rick," I made the corn ask me, "who do you hate more than anyone else? Try to see that person. Show us how you feel." I closed my eyes and tried to dissolve into tears, but the person I hated more than anyone else was me, and I couldn't see pummeling myself in the cornfield. My performances on stage became an endurance test, and I couldn't wait to talk to my acting teacher when I got back to New York. I'd tell her what a failure I'd been.

"I didn't feel anything," I bravely proclaimed back in Greenwich Village. "I don't have an emotional life. I can't act."

My dear teacher must have resisted a strong impulse to say, "What utter rot!" Instead, she replied, "Rick, why don't you sing for us?" That I *could* do. I picked a very sentimental ballad. Not daring to look at any of my classmates, I sang to the spotlights burning down on me. I didn't have to conjure up images of conflicts with my parents or a crisis of personal inadequacy. The song itself spoke of love and loss and a melancholy I felt deeply. By the time I finished singing, I was visibly moved. I usually was when I sang. Why had I never noticed that before?

"See, you feel," my teacher told me. "I saw it in your face, and I felt it. Tell me the names for some of the emotions you felt."

"Love."

"What else?"

"Despair, maybe."

"And?"

"Anger, sorrow, hope."

"Yes, I think they were all there."

No, the class wasn't therapy. It wasn't meant to be. Still, it served a wonderful purpose in my life. I was asked to feel, and I was asked to find names for how I felt. This can be an incredibly frustrating process at first, just like closing your eyes in prayer and hearing nothing more than the hum of the air-conditioning unit and the buzz of the fluorescent lights. Gradually, though, it got a little easier and started making more sense. Because of my acting class I began paying more attention to how people said what they said, asking myself why they said it. I started to see how an answer such as "Nothing" to the question "What's wrong?" can mean a dozen things more complicated than "Nothing." I began to look for the feelings of characters in plays. And when I asked myself the actor's proverbial question, "What's my motivation?" I started to ask Rick Hamlin the same thing.

What *was* my motivation? Most of the time, I had to confess, it was to be loved, to be appreciated, to be needed, to be adored. I was pretty good at constructing defenses to shield that truth from most of the people I met, but there it was, on the indoor-outdoor carpeting, in the glare of the spotlights: I wanted to be loved.

I discovered what a bad liar I was. I suspect most of us are. How frustrating God must find it, listening to us get our wants all wrong, hearing us ask for the new house, the better car (if we can be that honest), the job with more prestige, the good tennis game, when what we really want is to be loved. I was no different. I thought I wanted things that would give me the power to impress. Instead, I just wanted to be loved.

"You wanted to be loved?" inquired my spiritual director.

"Yes."

"Had you ever realized that about yourself before?"

"Perhaps, but that was the first time I'd articulated it clearly. That was when I first discovered that the need for love was such a motivating factor in my life."

"So few people know that about themselves," he observed. "When I give speeches on the dinner-party circuit, it's the one theme I know will captivate any audience. It's the one thing everyone has in common, rich and poor alike."

I looked at him a little differently. He was just like me. *He* wanted to be loved. "I was scared to admit it," I said. "I still find it hard to acknowledge at times."

"What did you do about it back then?"

"It's not that I did anything; it's what it did for me."

In New York my "day job" was a night job at the now defunct
Hotel Winslow. I was a desk clerk on the four-to-midnight
shift. At that time the hotel had only thirty permanent residents, all of whom the owners were trying to relocate. The
structure was being transformed into an office building. My
job was mindless and boring. I sat for hours underneath a few
bald lightbulbs, distributing packages and mail to a handful of
elderly residents who believed against the evidence that they
could stay on in the aging building, one tenant to a floor. I had
long hours to myself, to study scripts, write letters, and chat on
the phone to friends. The hotel residents, in threadbare coats
and moth-eaten hats, would linger in the empty lobby, sitting
on the rattling radiators and making polite conversation as
though their world weren't crumbling around them.

As most actors' "money jobs" went, it could have been
worse. I found plenty of time to memorize scenes for my acting class, learn music, and read through three different daily
newspapers. From the front desk I watched the drama of
everyday life pass through the shabby lobby: a Russian expatri-
ate cinematographer looking in vain for some news from
home, an impoverished French diplomat's wife waiting for an
inheritance that never seemed to come, a middle-aged Belgian

"nurse" who did more lucrative business at night as a call girl, a Cuban refugee always rushing to Saint Patrick's Cathedral with her rosary beads in hand, and friends of mine who stopped by on their way home from their more conventional nine-to-five jobs.

One of those friends was a college chum who worked in publishing. She was compiling a calendar of quotations—a provocative quote a day—and to earn some extra money I dutifully retyped the manuscript. She was at a transition point in her career and in her life. She knew she could get a job that earned her more than her publishing salary, or she could earn a lot less and take a risk by doing what she really wanted to do, which was to be a freelance writer. She'd recently forgone the Talbot sweaters and khaki skirts of college days; now, with hair flamboyantly hennaed red, she dressed in Bohemian black or outrageous purple, and on rainy days she wore a trendy translucent raincoat. She rolled her eyes at the motley crew assembled in the lobby and issued sharp, opinionated views on the New York cultural scene. Of course, I advised her on her job quandary. "You should be a writer," I told her. Easy for me to say. She'd had some success with an authoritative tome on fingernails; other successes would surely follow. But the real point I was trying to make was, "You should do what you want to do."

"How do I make money in the meantime?" she asked, ever practical.

"I'm sure I could get you a job here at the hotel," I said. So she left her publishing job and took over the 8:00 A.M. shift, working on her manuscripts at the front desk. I usually came early for my 4:00 P.M. shift, or she lingered, so that we could talk. She was great fun to talk to. Witty, clever, she had strong opinions about everything. Moreover, she gave me the feeling that the things I said were witty and clever too. In the gossip and banter, sometimes subjects of great seriousness would suddenly emerge. I thought it odd one afternoon when she bit her lip, avoided my gaze—perhaps afraid that I would be censorious—and announced, "You'll never know what a difference you've made in my life."

It seemed such a curious cliché from a woman who scorned anything that faintly resembled cheap sentiment. "No, I guess I won't," I mumbled then, not knowing what she was referring to. But the brave acknowledgment of some feeling, some hidden depth of understanding between two people who pretended to be aloof to raw emotions, was an invitation. We were good friends, we had a good time together, we enjoyed each other's company, and now we were teetering on the edge of something that threatened to do in a good friendship. When we talked about books, we weren't really thinking about the books; when the movies came up, we weren't wholly analyzing their strengths and weaknesses; when we gossiped about friends, we had another scenario in mind.

Maybe I should have known from earlier signals. Once when she was away for two weeks on vacation I house-sat at her apartment. When I got restless at night, I'd search under her sink for ammonia and cleanser and take to the windows and walls, attacking hidden spots like the top of the refrigerator, the narrow area behind the john, and the smudges on the telephone. (I also untangled the phone cord by hanging it out the skyscraper window.) She blushed in embarrassment when she returned, shaking her head and muttering, "I can't believe you washed my phone!" as though I had scored a touchdown with only seconds left in the fourth quarter. And there was the Sunday brunch she arranged so that I could meet her best friend—a brunch at which she served a shad roe omelette that I didn't eat much of. Afterward she told me how much her best friend liked me, as if I were somebody who had to be inspected, my jawline checked out for any flaws, my teeth examined like a horse's. Did I count in some unexpected way?

Then there was the bright winter morning when we went to a piano warehouse downtown and I bought the cheapest instrument we could find, firewood that I would later pay someone to take away. As we walked side by side in the bitter cold, our breath blowing behind us as if we were two steamships climbing the Hudson, everything seemed magnified: my delight in the day, the rashness of spending several hundred dollars in one fell swoop, the crush of her parka when she brushed against my wool overcoat. My perceptions were heightened, and something as mundane as the steam billowing through the holes in a manhole cover seemed as magnificent as Old Faithful. What did this mean?

Growing often involves giving up what's familiar for the unknown. It can mean going from what's comfortable and reassuring into a dark and forbidding void. After all, you don't know if happiness lies beyond where you are until you've traveled there. For both of us the risks were enormous. It would have been easier if we were strangers drawn to each other, but proven and time-tested "affection" and "warmth" were such risky things to give up for an unknown quantity like love. I used to tell myself, "I can imagine us being great friends when we're old and retired, but I can't fathom our relationship when we're grown-up thirty-year-olds." We could visualize a future together of comfortable fondness—like gray-haired siblings at an old folks' home—but it was too threatening to imagine being together boyfriend and girlfriend, committed, in love.

Conveniently enough, or inconveniently, I decided to try my luck as an actor in California. I was feeling only half-committed to the profession, and half-committed is even less than half of what it takes to survive the hustling, the penury, the hassles, and the rejection that always feels personal even though you repeatedly try to convince yourself that it isn't. As an actor you're supposed to be sensitive and vulnerable, but after enough of "Thanks—don't call us, we'll call you," you realize a greater asset would be a thick hide. So professionally and emotionally, I was ready to try the geographic cure. I could still call myself an actor in California and probably get some work, but I would also be a few thousand miles away from someone I wanted to see more than reason allowed.

The night before I was to leave New York, she invited me to her place for dinner. There, far above the traffic noise, with nothing but a view of midtown Manhattan lights (no room to put a picture on the wall), she cooked liver in onions—it was cheap—and I munched on potato chips. The winter wind blew through the cracks in the uneven casement windows, she sneezed again and again from a terrible cold, and we kept conversation going rapidly about everything but us. It was as though we were cartoon figures stepping off a cliff, suspended in midair without knowing it. If either of us had looked down, we would have plummeted—a free fall. Falling in love can be made to sound so romantic afterward, but it can be utter torture when it's happening. Neither of us could bring ourselves to say that maybe . . . perhaps . . . it was possible . . .

"You need to get up early tomorrow," I said, trying to excuse myself with the convenient cover of politeness.

"And you probably have to do Christmas shopping, or something like that."

"Something like that." I gave her a friendly kiss—a kiss on the cheek. There was some hesitation, a momentary fluster, an awful awkwardness.

"We'll talk," I said, trying to recover.

"Yes. Okay. We'll talk."

Sometimes it's awful to contemplate what might have happened, terrible to imagine what could have resulted if I had not or she had not done this or that. It makes for agonizing daydreams. How right the sentimental soul who declared, "'What might have been'—the four saddest words in the English language." When I look on this moment in my life, I squirm uncomfortably. I can barely read the letters I wrote to Carol back then, because they're filled with the hidden fear that things would not work out all right. All my tentative, hesitant, self-conscious yearnings are there beneath the arch meandering.

What if she hadn't written that first brave letter making the first courageous declaration that we were falling in love? What if I hadn't responded to her letter with a paragraph (rewritten countless times) conceding that maybe, perhaps, she was right? Yes, we were falling in love, and doing it in the best, time-honored Victorian fashion. We joked on the page about publishing the whole lurid correspondence—a limited edition with lavender endpapers—but I can't imagine that anyone would find a romantic, inspiring word in it. There certainly was never a spontaneous thought. Every feeling, every emotion, every whim went down on paper only after it had been analyzed and edited to death. Sometimes whole paragraphs were rewritten and copied onto a new sheet of stationery. We took risks by baby steps, revealing ourselves in asides and then backing up and saying, "Of course, that might not be true."

For months we lived for those letters, sometimes three or four a week, single-spaced, several pages long. I could hardly wait for the letter carrier to call. Whenever I came home, I looked for those typed letters with the address written in a southpaw's backward scrawl, in a fountain pen's blue ink. I opened them and read them slowly, savoring each sentence, my heart beating rapidly in case she had changed her mind over something she had previously said. We were always two or three letters behind in our responses, giving us time to catch up with our thoughts as the mail crossed the continent. We enjoyed discovering who we were on the page, because even if we were ever so careful, we were also honest. We were open in a guarded way. We learned to read each other's minds between the lines. We allowed ourselves to love a little. All the while we made but a few long-distance calls for fear that the immediacy of the voice would send us both back to our clever, aloof, distanced selves.

Did I pray to God for any of this to happen? Hardly. I was too afraid. I couldn't allow myself even to fantasize that the love I was being offered could be real and long-lasting. I could accept it only from letter to letter, from tentative step to tentative step. For four months I stayed in California and we wrote to each other. She talked about religion. She described a sermon she had heard that had touched her. It was about Mary, the mother of Christ, and how this young, inexperienced girl could be chosen for such an enormous role. The minister took the occasion to talk about God's calling—and how God calls each of us and can help us do far more than we think we're capable of if we only accept what we're asked to do. God can help us even if we make mistakes. He's helpless only if we do nothing—which Carol and I were both quite aware was the danger we faced with this fierce love we had discovered. God could never help us if we did nothing, if we let apathy and the two thousand miles of distance separating us take their course.

In another letter Carol talked about going into a Manhattan church at midday to pray after she had been severely tempted to start up a relationship with someone else. She didn't say whether the prayer had helped. She didn't mention if the temptation had been successfully squelched—but there it was, as backhanded an acknowledgment of commitment as ever there was. She was telling me how important I was to her. What would I do about it?

I ask myself now (and I wondered then), Why should it be so hard to accept love? I'd already admitted to myself that love was what I wanted more than anything else, and now that it was being offered, I could barely bring myself to say yes.

At the time I was doing children's theater. Driving from one elementary school to another, our troupe put on a forty-five-minute-long play for squirming, squealing kids. Sometimes we did three or four performances a day, putting up the set and taking it down at each auditorium, gym, or sloppy-joe-stained cafeteria. At the end of a long day my voice would be hoarse and my back weary from carrying the set. My fellow cast members were a good-natured bunch, but they couldn't understand what attraction New York held for me. Why live in that stinking hole when, living in Southern California, you could drive to Hollywood in the morning for an audition and surf that afternoon? I was beginning to wonder if they were right. After one hundred performances, we were given Easter week off. This was my time to find out.

"I can't really afford it," I told a friend, "but I probably should fly back to New York for the week to visit a girl I might be in love with."

My friend didn't hesitate. "I'll give you the money for the trip," he said, though at the time he didn't have any money to throw around. With that I knew I had to go. Friends have a way of forcing you to do the things you want to do anyway, giving you the courage to do them.

I took the red-eye flight on Saturday night, arriving at Kennedy Airport on Palm Sunday morning. The grass was that pale-green color that's called "spring green" on children's crayons. The blossoms on the tulip trees looked like limp toilet paper, and the daffodils leaned against a cold wind. Before anyone else was awake, Carol and I sat near the rowing pond in Central Park and watched the ducks waddle through the mud and the sun break out behind pink clouds above a limestone-sheathed apartment building. We both managed to say, "I missed you." It was much harder to say, "I love you."

For a week—Holy Week, no less—we did all those frivolous, romantic, two-on-the-town things New York offers young lovers in the spring. We walked through museums hand in hand, went to movies in the middle of the day, sat in Central Park in the fuzzy sun, ate hearty breakfasts at Greek delis. I bought a pair of overpriced linen pants at a Madison Avenue boutique and was coaxed into paying for a jaunty Panama hat, wearing it even though it was out of season. We lingered in bookstores, window-shopped when the money ran out, took cover in hotel lobbies from the occasional shower, and drank big mugs of hot tea.

We went to visit her mother in Connecticut one day, I guess so I could be inspected. Afterward I wrote the obligatory thank-you note. I said something to the effect that I looked forward to seeing her again "when my ship comes in." Carol's mother wrote me back, a thank-you note for a thank-you note, saying, "Don't wait too long. Ships are notoriously late coming in."

All the while in New York we hid from our friends, once literally darting behind a newsstand when we saw a former Princeton classmate. We had enough trouble admitting to each other we were in love; it would have been far too threatening to admit it to anyone else. We both sensed that for our love to grow it needed to be kept a secret; it was too young, too delicate, too tender, a seed germinating in the dark. In the Sermon on the Mount Jesus told his listeners to pray in isolation, literally in a closet. Perhaps that was meant as an exhortation against flamboyant demonstrations of holiness—but it also must have had something to do with the fragile nature of our deepest longings. There comes a time when our dreams can be exposed and they blossom before a crowd, but at first they find power and strength in privacy. Some prayers are meant only for God's ears, even after they've been answered.

No, there was no need to pray that week. Love letters and love poems are never written when you're with the object of your desires; impassioned pleas for happiness don't need to be made when indescribable bliss has made an unexpected appearance. It was rare enough for two usually self-conscious people to give up analyzing and articulating their every feeling. The future was confusing enough. For a week we just enjoyed the present. Finally, though, on a rainy Easter Sunday, the week came to an end and I had to return to California and resume performances for loud, jaded schoolchildren in Orange County. When would we see each other again? Whose turn was it to make the next move? Who would visit whom, and where?

This is the worst part to remember. This is when I squirm most. This is the part my memory would rather glide right past. I was so craven, so timid. I can torture myself even now by wondering, What if it hadn't turned out all right? What might have been? Pride is a strong emotion and doubly powerful when coupled with fear. Pride justifies fear, wraps it up in excuses that sound legitimate. I could have quit the exhausting children's show and returned to New York, where I knew I was meant to be. But I told myself I wasn't going to alter my career for a girl. That would be a bad start to things. Maybe I wanted to see how much I counted. Maybe I was testing her. Maybe we did indeed need to wait for "the fullness of time."

At any rate, there was a miserable year of phone calls, letters, transcontinental flights, and interminable waiting as we tried to decide who we were to each other. That summer I was singing the lead in *West Side Story* in Santa Barbara, and Carol came out to visit at the end of the run. In August the water off Santa Barbara's coast was unusually clear, with visibility of thirty or forty feet. You could see the rocks, the purple kelp, and the white sandy bottom. But Carol swam in the ocean with trepidation. She said she preferred the murky water of Long Island Sound, where in waist-high water she couldn't see her toes. I saw that as a metaphor for where we stood. I didn't like clarity; I preferred murkiness; I didn't want to see as far as a clear future.

I wasn't unoccupied while I waited—waited, that is, for my actions to catch up with my emotions. I formally gave up being an actor and decided to call myself something else. I would be a writer—as though giving myself the title were enough. I got a part-time job with a Hollywood production office as a Boy Friday and all-around "gofer," starting my shift at two in the afternoon so that I could write in the morning. At least it was a way of taking time for myself, almost like painting my sister's house. I drove in the morning to one of the parks in the arroyo and sat at a picnic table under sycamores and eucalyptus trees, watching the dew lift and the fog turn into smog.

Those mornings in the local parks brought back my boyhood, the fragrance of eucalyptus, the merry-go-rounds that made me throw up, the carob seedpods and live oak acorns I had collected, the sandbox castles I'd built. As I wrote, I tried to trust the images of my imagination. I wrote a novel, something I've never reread and have never asked another soul to look at. When I finished it, I was ready to give up whatever prevented me from doing what I wanted to do. I was ready to love and be loved. I was ready to stop waiting.

I should have got down on bended knee by the time I returned to New York. I should have scripted a long, dramatic, romantic proposal. But in fact the marriage proposal had to be coaxed or embarrassed out of me by another friend. *O Lord, was I that passive? Was I so craven?*

Carol and I were out at her mother's house in Connecticut with our mutual friend Steve. We took him on a tour through the picturesque New England town where she'd grown up, passing the school she'd attended, the library where she'd read for endless summer afternoons, the village green, the main street, and finally the church where she'd worshiped.

As we passed it, Steve, who has a gift for being blessedly blunt, said, "If you two were to get married—say, to each other—would you get married there?"

"Not in that church," Carol said, and we both blushed. "I'd prefer to get married in New York."

Later, when we were treading water in my future mother-in-law's pool, I said, "Well, what about it?"

She said, "Well?"

"Well, what? Do you want to get married?"

"Of course. I wondered when you were finally going to ask me."

"I was waiting for you to say you were ready."

"I was waiting for you to *be* ready."

Well, we were ready.

"So you wrote love letters," observed my spiritual director.

"That's how we courted. Yes."

"What a help for you in your prayer life."

"How's that?"

"They taught you how to wait. You knew what it was to express yourself when all you had to go on was hope. You learned how to take big risks when you couldn't see the face of the one you loved and couldn't know what her reaction was. You had to trust. You had to accept her response on faith. A prayer can be a love letter to God, pouring out your soul."

I could see his point, all those letters back and forth where we had to accept each other's word on faith. But I had to disagree in part. My prayers were never as tentative and canned as those letters to Carol. My prayers were never so wordy. In fact, they often didn't include words, just inchoate thoughts and deep feelings that I would never have been able to express if I had had to. "I've been more honest in prayer than I ever was writing love letters," I said.

"But look at the resolution of all that letter writing. You learned what it is to be loved and to love in return. You gave of yourself and you gained a partner for life. No one can develop fully without being understood and appreciated by one other person. You found a relationship, an earthly version of the great spiritual one. That's why we use the term 'relationship with God' or 'relationship with Jesus Christ'; that's what we're thinking about."

And yet being married to Carol didn't seem to help me in my struggle with my work. I wasn't instantly led to my vocation. I still wasn't certain what I was meant to be doing. I feared that I was floundering.

That first year of marriage other young married couples often came up to us and asked, in grave tones (as though we were recovering from a serious illness), "How's it going? How is it to be married? You know, the first year is the hardest."

Hard? It was as easy as falling off a log. Being married seemed the only logical, sensible thing I'd done since graduating from college. Sure, you can act like you're giving up everything, making a sacrifice greater than any saint's, willing to live as a committee the rest of your days. You can pretend to be a martyr because you had to give up your own private identity for the sake of a shared one. But if it's the right person, you find that you're not really giving up anything after all. I was never very good at being a bachelor anyway.

I loved saying the word *wife* to myself. It amused me no end to refer to Carol as "my wife." I couldn't get over the novelty of wearing a wedding ring, the gold clanking against any hard object I picked up with my left hand, reminding me of my new status. In Italy on our honeymoon, I thought we could pass as any normal couple. Instead, every time we checked into a new hotel or *pensione*, someone at the front desk would smile coyly and ask, "*Sposini? Luna di miele?*" "Newlyweds? On your honeymoon?" I was a member of the club, this not-so-secret society that made everyone smile, everyone wink, everyone laugh. I was happy. I delighted in this new identity, this unexpected pleasure of belonging.

But with this new responsibility, what I found hard was facing the perception others had of me (and I had myself) that I wasn't . . . well . . . doing anything important.

"Mr. Hamlin," the society reporter from the *New York Times* who was writing up our marriage announcement had asked, "Mr. Hamlin, are you still a . . . writer?" I could hear the snotty scorn in his voice. How dare I presume so much about myself? "Are you working for anyone? Have you published any books yet?"

No, I hadn't. But it wasn't for want of trying.

That first year of marriage I sat at my typewriter in the living room and she sat at hers in the office/bedroom of our tiny apartment. Every day we wrote. I could hear her typewriter go clickety-clack at an intimidating pace—eleven pages before lunch—while I hunted and pecked my way through another turgid manuscript, another piece deserving of the form rejection slip that came back in the stamped, self-addressed envelope. That first year I earned a couple of thousand dollars from my pen, but it didn't compensate for my low self-esteem. I wondered if I should go back to being an actor/singer again. Maybe I could earn some money. Heck, a woman on the subway, seeing me study a Gilbert and Sullivan score for an amateur production, gave me her card, said she was an agent, and asked me to come by her office. That had never happened when I was knocking on every agent's door from Fifty-seventh Street to Forty-second.

What made things so hard was that I felt surrounded by confidence. When I used the research library in midtown Manhattan, I could see young men and women who looked like my friends walking purposefully from subway to office, briefcase in hand, their faces strained with thoughts of meetings, presentations, legal briefs, documents, and fleeting arguments with managers and colleagues. I called my old college chums at their offices, and women old enough to be their mothers referred to them by their surnames: Mr. Rich, Mr. Hilboldt, Mr. Byrns. When did we grow up? Or were we just faking it? Had I missed the boat?

Eating lunch by myself, I could sit on the library steps and watch the yuppie procession pass—the coats left back at the office, the windblown ties flying over one shoulder like would-be scarves. I eavesdropped on conversations about public offerings, marketing strategies, and ad campaigns. Over lunch with my friends I would try to make the budding lawyers tell me about cases they couldn't talk about, hearing them refer to clients anonymously as "a well-known international corporation headquartered in Cleveland" or "a Third World country that needs to refinance its massive debt." Sometimes their faces became curiously rigid and their expressions unanimated, as though I were the boss or the managing partner. I marveled at their sangfroid in office disputes, their political machinations, their ambition and determination, but I didn't envy them their work. I didn't want to market toothpaste or stay up all night at the printer's to proof a public offering.

One evening, as I listened to my wife talk about publishing a book of hers, I felt hopelessly out of it. I had no direction. I was a failure. She had all the smooth self-assurance that I lacked. That night on our futon, after she had fallen asleep, I scribbled furiously in my journal and I cried in my pillow. I was at the end of my rope. *Lord,* I prayed, *what do you want me to do?*

That night I had a dream, as mixed up and muddled as most of my dreams. I was at church in the choir loft, wearing my choir robe, and down in the pulpit preaching was a young female assistant, a woman not much older than I was. I knew her well. Her husband had been trained as a pastor too, but he'd gone on to become a pastoral counselor, then a professional therapist. Susan was speaking from the pulpit in my dream, and as I listened to her, I heard a Godlike voice inside me say, "Be like Susan's husband."

I woke up in the dark on our futon, the dream as vivid as a movie just seen. I sat up for a few minutes, alert, so I'd be sure to remember it in the daylight. "Be like Susan's husband" was the important message. I wouldn't forget it. And I returned to sleep, rested, calm, not certain what the dream meant but confident of a path to follow to figure it out.

The next day I made an appointment with Susan to talk. My wife seemed pleased: I was doing something that seemed practical. When I met with Susan she served me some herbal tea and fed her five-month-old infant as I recounted the dream. Between burping the baby and warming the bottle, Susan asked me, with an enigmatic smile, "Was this dream a . . . mystical experience?"

What a flattering question! Oh, to think that the gods might be so generous with me! How I would have loved to be shown a simple, direct path, as in one of the visions of prophets and saints. Had I experienced something mystical? I stared up at the high ceiling in the overheated room and wondered.

Then reality intruded, as mundane as the beep of the microwave announcing that the baby's formula was warm. No, the heavens hadn't opened up. The dream wasn't a godly recipe. It felt like all my other dreams: pieces of half-baked thoughts and images gathering in a confused narrative of my subconscious mind. Just as my father had graciously never told me exactly what profession to follow or what job to take, God wasn't dictating to me. It wasn't a cosmic order. But there was something persuasive about the dream, as though one of God's angels had tapped me on the shoulder.

"No, it wasn't mystical. But it was important enough not to dismiss. It made me think. That's why I'm here." And then I asked the big question on my mind: "How do we know what God wants us to do?"

"There are many ways." We talked then a lot about spiritual things, interrupted only by the cooing baby on the couch. And it dawned on me that this was the first time I'd told Susan or anyone that I somehow believed God wanted me to be someone special or do something special and that I wanted to figure out what it was.

Susan, never one for quick, pat answers, suggested prayer and study and talking to other people. I took the least intimidating approach—talking to other people.

First I talked to Susan's husband. He told me what a therapist did and how one became a psychologist, and neither the necessary education nor the profession appealed to me. Next I talked to a minister who had been a college classmate. He mentioned prayer and Bible study too. Then he handed me a thin devotional book as I was leaving his office. I shelved it back at home. I talked to other friends as well. I asked them how they had settled on a vocation and whether God had had anything to do with it. They pursed their lips, shook their wise heads, and said, in effect, "I figured I could find something on my own." More followers of the doctrine that God helps those who help themselves.

I was grateful for the advice. I wanted someone else to be right about my life. I wanted to find the one fortune-teller who would give me a forecast I agreed upon. If only the decision making could be taken out of my hands. If only the secret plot with the satisfying denouement could be found in a word, a book, a fortune cookie.

Finally a friend suggested his godfather, who also happened to be a minister. He had been very kind to my friend, so I was disposed to like him. "He'll help you sort things out."

That man, that minister, that godfather became my spiritual director. And he did that odd thing: he didn't dismiss the vocational question. He heard what I said and brought it back to something more central. "Do you know God?" he had said.

"Why is that important?" I finally asked after several sessions.

"Because if you're concerned about doing what God wants you to do, you should at least start out by knowing God. Do you know God?"

The television in the next room kept blaring, children nearby continued their boisterous playing, cars outside honked, a clock on the mantelpiece ticked. The question embarrassed me. I would have preferred to be cavalier, offhand, slightly sarcastic in my response, but it was too serious a question to duck. I paused. I started to ramble. Then I went back to pausing.

The pause went on for many months, and many visits, when we talked about prayer and I reported on my progress. You've read about that time already. I've tried to describe it both as I remember it now and as I remembered it while it was happening.

During one of our visits, when I had sunk into some sort of profound silence about the ineffable, the minister told me *his* story.

"For fifteen years I read Scripture, I delivered sermons, I prayed, I organized rummage sales, I ran parish meetings, I taught, I studied—and for those fifteen years I didn't really know God. And then I faced a personal crisis."

(I smiled at that—"personal crisis" was such minister language.)

"And in that personal crisis, I prayed, I doubted, I felt lost. I was almost ready to give up being a minister; I felt like an impostor. And then one morning, when I was reading the psalms and came across the passage in the forty-sixth psalm that talks about the city of God and how God is in the midst of her, I felt deeply moved. Maybe because I was in the midst of the city and that's where I had made my ministry. At that moment I experienced a strange calm. I knew that God existed, that Jesus was his son, and that he loved me."

He could have been talking about Paul on the road to Damascus, or John Wesley feeling his heart "strangely warmed" while listening to a reading of Martin Luther's preface to Romans, or even the testimony of some TV evangelist who could name the exact date and time—down to the illuminated seconds on the clock-radio dial—when "the Lord Jesus Christ entered my life." It was a phenomenon as old as time, and the boldness of it, the shopworn vocabulary, the prepackaged glory made me uncomfortable.

"What do you suggest I do?" I asked timidly.

He'd stopped looking at me. He was fishing around in his desk for something and probably glancing sideways at his watch to see if it was time for his next appointment, his next searching soul. Then he looked up, almost surprised to see me still there.

"Open up your heart. Look. Listen. God will find anyone who looks hard for him."

I did what I usually do. I went searching for stories, this time from friends, to understand something of the divine.

For a long time Jim didn't believe in God. He'd grown up in a "rationalistic" household. His parents were both scientists, brilliant Ph.D.'s. On Sunday mornings they drove him to the nearby Unitarian Church and dropped him off at Sunday school so that he'd know something about religion, but they didn't believe in anything more than a deistic concept of God, a mathematical construct that must have been hard to pray to.

"The only way I knew anything about faith was through the Bible my grandmother gave me," Jim said.

That Bible sat for a long time on a shelf full of economic textbooks, business law journals, and his wife's novels. Only as a young father did Jim take down the Bible and start reading the Gospels. They filled him with a desire to believe. He longed to have faith like that of the woman who was cured by touching the hem of Christ's cloak, or faith like that of Thomas, who in the end didn't have to touch the wounds in Jesus' hands to believe that he was the risen Christ, or even faith like that of the bumbling Peter, whose zeal continually got him in trouble. For over a year Jim's work took him to a small, bleak Iowa city during the week, away from his wife and children. On long lonely nights in his rented apartment close to the train tracks, where he could hear the mournful howl of freight trains rumbling past, he turned to that Bible.

"But I still didn't believe," he said. "I read the Bible and went to church on Sundays with my family, but I couldn't quite accept something I couldn't see or feel or touch. Intellectually I came to a point where I could acknowledge God's existence, but emotionally I didn't know God at all." (He sounded like me.)

Then came the night of the dream. He'd been on the phone that evening, planning a church trip to the ballpark, lining up people, trying to get enough names to fill a block of seats. That night when he fell asleep, he dreamed about the ballpark. The group from church was in a lounge skybox, one of those expensive corporate clubhouses that provide tax-deductible perks for business entertainment, with a wet bar and a television and a great view of the game. Jim's church group sat on sofas, looking down at the green field.

Suddenly Jim felt the urge to leave. He had to go on some vague errand. He promised the group that he would be back. Next thing he knew he was running along a tree-shaded street near his church. He was moving very fast, almost at the speed of a car. He turned a sharp, gravelly corner and his legs slipped out from under him. As he started to fall, he feared that because of his high speed he would be killed on the hard asphalt. Just then he was picked up and carried, borne above the ground by strong arms. He felt safe. He was loved and cared for. He was protected.

"I understood even while the dream was happening that this was God rescuing me. He cared about me, loved me, knew me," Jim said. "I was left with such an intimate feeling of comfort, warmth, and protection. It was a sense of well-being. I was absolutely at peace. I knew that if I died, no harm would come to me. I was in God's arms."

When he told me this story, I asked if it was the only time he had had such a mystical feeling. Was once enough? Yes, once was indeed enough. But there had been another occasion. Smaller, a fleeting feeling, like a wave passing over a sandy beach and quickly retreating, changing the landscape nevertheless. It happened one evening when he was lying in bed with his wife, both of them reading. Suddenly he felt vulnerable and exposed. He realized how helpless he was on his own. He leaned over and held on to his wife, embracing her. *I know that feeling too,* I thought. *I've felt that sureness, that closeness, that holy satisfaction.*

"But the weird thing was," he said, "I knew I was embracing more than her. I sensed that at that moment I was also, in a weird, mystical way, holding my arms around God."

He shrugged his shoulders and smiled as he said it, like one who knows that well-constructed, intellectual arguments can never explain what the heart believes. He was embarrassed because before he'd had the experience and the dream, he wouldn't have believed such stories from someone else. Logical, careful with words, practical, the kind of man who saves for his daughters' college education when they're barely out of the womb, he'd suddenly embraced the absurd.

Then there was Claire.

I knew about Claire in college because she was older and glamorous, a campus star. After graduation she made her way out to Hollywood and quickly became a studio vice president. When I was a struggling actor in California and going through the misery of no one returning my telephone calls, I sent my photo and résumé to Claire's office, explaining that I was a friend of a friend. After leaving a couple of messages, I received a call from her secretary, who promised that Claire would receive me at 2:05 the next Thursday. She was doing this supreme favor "not because of Princeton," I was told, but because of our mutual friend (oh, the power in the right name).

The office reeked of Hollywood, with thick green carpets, bamboo print wallpaper, a white upholstered sofa, framed film posters, and a small refrigerator from which the secretary took out a bottle of fizzy mineral water, pouring me some in a crystal glass. But Claire herself didn't seem very Hollywood. Pretty, vulnerable, and absolutely sincere. She set up an appointment for me with the studio's casting department and was honest about my limited chances. (This was one instance where I refrained from volunteering all my potential failings as an actor.)

We ran into each other again a year later in California at a church gathering when I was no longer an actor and she was about to leave the studio. Sunday morning's guest speaker, she spoke candidly about the failure of Hollywood to deliver films that improved people's lives or addressed inner needs, and she described the beginnings of her own spiritual search. That search ultimately took her along a torturous path that veered off into half a dozen religions, not to mention several health therapies (this *was* Southern California). Fiercely intelligent, intellectually adroit, she left making movies to be able to read, meditate, study, and pray while living a more precarious hand-to-mouth life. She stoutly maintained that while all religions seemed to reflect aspects of the godly light—as the moon reflects the sun—she was searching to know the light itself.

And then one day she had an experience that changed her forever. She had been praying and fasting, following a Native American rite that involved long periods in a steam hut. (As I write this, I'm aware of my inability to understand and describe the nuances of the ritual.) She had the day to wander through the fragrant, arid California foothills, and in the heightened awareness that often comes with prayer, she sat down on a granite boulder, staring at an ant.

The ant seemed confused. As if trapped in a shallow depression in the rock, it wandered around in circles, back and forth, down and across, marking but never leaving its circumscribed fortress. It could easily have escaped the warming granite, but it couldn't choose one path. It searched for a route but wouldn't follow any of the choices available. It baked on the rock as though surrounded by concrete walls.

"That's me," Claire thought. *That's me too*, I thought when I heard the story. Exploring all the options, she couldn't commit to one religion. She remained a prisoner of her own intellect. She couldn't take the necessary leap of faith, catapulting over those walls. And because of it, she was circling in her own path, like Winnie the Pooh and Piglet wandering around the same tree again and again, more frightened every time they saw their own footsteps. *God can help you if you make a mistake, but he can do nothing for you if you're indecisive.*

Claire made a decision that day. She made a commitment. She chose one path—a path that took her out of her intellectual self. She finally gave herself to faith. And that's what I was finding it very difficult to do.

Here I was, Sunday morning's star tenor, warbling the doxology in the choir loft, reciting every word of the creeds. I loved the stories Jesus told; I loved the feeling I got when I prayed; I loved the glorious music of a Sunday morning worship service and the communion of saints in the liturgy. I liked church potluck suppers and stewardship campaigns. God forgive me, I even liked church committee meetings. But I didn't really believe half of what I heard, recited, or sang.

One day after church I was standing in the sun on the steps, amid the noise of the honking cabs and screeching buses, and I turned to my friend Jeffrey, as worldly and wise as any friend I've got. He buys his suits at Paul Stuart and writes elegant stories for glossy magazines. He's an expert at things I don't know how to handle, like getting a good table at a restaurant and returning telephone calls to publicists. A regular churchgoer, he's no starry-eyed, Bible-thumping, Spirit-moved Christian, but altogether sensible and practical. I figured he would have the straight goods on Jesus. So that day on the church steps I asked him if he really bought it all, hook, line, and sinker.

"Frederick," he said—the only one of my friends to call me by my christened name—"Frederick, you believe it or you don't. But if you don't, you might as well not be here."

I was there and he was there (and he wasn't even being paid to be there, as I was).

When I listened to Jim or Claire or even Jeffrey, I distrusted the *neatness* of believing. I was reminded of those long, drawn-out narratives of people who had sinned on drugs and drink and sex and then suddenly found God and everything was okay. The instant turnaround, the quick change of direction, the crystal-clear insight—those plot devices bothered me. Oh, the new believer might start with a disclaimer such as this: "Things didn't get better overnight. I struggled, yet now I had God on my side." But such people's stories were notoriously void of details about the postconversion struggle. The dramatic turnaround was the climax. That and maybe two more getting-high-on-God paragraphs.

And then something happened to me . . .

(I wish I could say this to you in person, for you would see the smile on my face and note the way I express myself with bemused wonderment about what I don't understand. Perhaps it's just as well that we do this in print instead. I would make a horrible evangelist, a miserable soul-saver. I can't let go of the slight cynicism for long enough to take the smile off my face. Even when I tell the most bold-faced truth, I laugh as though it were a small white lie. I wear the shrug of the shoulders and crooked grin of the fabricator. So here, now, when I'm talking about the gravest mystery, you'll just have to take my word for it.)

A very sincere Christian friend wrote a letter asking me to pray for him. I wrote back, saying that yes indeed I would pray for him, although I wasn't sure about all this Jesus business or the workings of intercessory prayer.

"Boy, I thought *I* had problems," my friend wrote back. "But you've really got 'em! I'm going to be praying for you every day from now on."

My halting prayers for my friend probably laid the ground-work. When we pray for someone else, we're made vulnerable and compassionate. We become raw and broken; and when we're broken, we can finally be remade. Something extraordinary happens when we allow ourselves to be broken for someone else. I suspect a sort of spiritual energy passes through us; although I don't have the faintest idea how it does it, it can travel hundreds of miles through phone wires and the postal system and the atmosphere we breathe.

And then there was my friend's promise to pray for me. I was impressed, touched, warmed. My friend's prayers helped make me listen to what I needed to hear. They opened me up to the possibilities. A business consultant once told me that the hardest thing to do with his clients is to get them to listen and hear, *really hear*, the solutions his company can offer. Pinpointing the problem is relatively easy. Convincing a stuck-in-the-mud, slow-moving, bureaucratic corporation to turn on a dime is next to impossible. It takes hours of showing charts and pulling out graphs and looking at figures—all to get a person to listen. A single remark can change your whole life if you're tuned into it. If you're listening.

I wasn't listening very carefully that day at church. I was up in the choir loft, as usual, turning from leaflet to hymnal to anthem to psalm. I gave my ear to a fellow tenor whispering about his hangover from a party the night before and to another chorister excoriating the performance of a new diva at the Met. A visiting nun gave the sermon that day, and she had a small voice that didn't travel very well to the back of the chancel. I tuned in, began really *listening*, only when she came to her final prayer. (It would be about time to turn to a new hymn and then another anthem.)

Then she said these shocking (to me) words: "In Jesus' name, our Creator, Redeemer, and Lover." *Creator, Redeemer, and Lover.* Creator, yes, of course; that referred to the creation story in Genesis. And Redeemer, that was about death on the cross, the rolled-away rock, and the empty tomb. Predictable enough. But Lover! That was about God alive and with me in such an intimate way it embarrassed me.

A dozen images went through my mind in the briefest second, a whole host of associations with the word *lover* (lowercase). I slept with my lover. I happened to be married to her. She cooked most of my meals—and I did the dishes. I gave her chocolate on Valentine's Day, took her to dinner for our anniversary, bought her nightgowns for her birthday that usually turned out to be the wrong size. She was the one who worried more than I did when I was sick and dreaded the day when I might die. She was the person whose approval mattered so much that I refrained from asking for it, and yet I drank it up like nectar when it came with sweet thank-yous if I took out the trash or polished the silver or balanced the checkbook without even being asked. She was why I rushed home at night and what made me happiest to roll out of bed in the morning.

Lover was a word for someone who met my deepest needs. My lover (lowercase again) was someone who knew me inside and out. My lover was the inspiration for all the songs I sang. What a metaphor for God! It seemed so right. It shocked me, amazed me, startled me, delighted me. That sort of companionship, that kind of partner, that Other who took greater delight in me than I took in myself: Lover.

My spiritual advisor might have explained to me that this notion of God as Lover was as old as the Song of Solomon ("O that you would kiss me with the kisses of your mouth") and was beautifully used by Saint John of the Cross in his explicit love poem to Christ ("One dark night, fired with love's urgent longings . . . "). But I didn't need any explanations.

The word sank into my subconscious mind and transformed my understanding. Maybe the next day, maybe two weeks later, I realized I was praying to this man, this Lover (uppercase), this mystery bigger than any name can hold, Son of God, Word Incarnate, Jesus. I hate the exclusiveness of the Jesus club, those who claim no prayer can be made without the closing "In Jesus' name," but I understand their enthusiasm. His whole life was a prayer.

Like the Russian peasant pilgrim who prayed over and over again, *Jesus Christ, have mercy on me, a miserable sinner,* I could repeat, "Jesus Christ, have mercy on me . . ." Jesus, Jesus, Jesus. Those were words that led me to forget myself and enter into a prayer that transcended all my petty needs. On the subway, if I closed my eyes and repeated those words, I wasn't praying out of want. No desires needed to be mentioned. *He knows the desires of the heart.* What a prayer! What a lover!

For our last meeting my spiritual director took me to his club for lunch. This felt right, just the kind of place for the society minister I had taken him to be. Through the unmarked doors with their polished brass handles we went, up the marble steps with the red carpet held flush by brass rods, stopping for drinks in a paneled room hung with Hudson River school landscapes. Mr. Spiritual Director, dwarfed in a wing chair that rose above his dark head like bat's ears, had a beer and I had some mineral water, popping peanuts into my mouth in between sips. Like a favorite high school teacher you visit after you've had a taste of "the real world," he suddenly seemed smaller, less clever, more ordinary, hardly insightful at all. He could have been an accountant in a bespoke suit, an auditor on an expense-account lunch. No clerical collar, no Buddha aura. This was my guru? This was the man who was my spiritual guide?

He listened to my latest spiritual revelations with his usual combination of intense concentration and impatience. Gazing about the room to see if any cronies had arrived, congregation-cruising, he turned to me. "Jesus will help you in your prayer life. Give you something to focus on."

I was reminded of a classic Rotary introduction. The guest speaker is sitting on the dais, and the club president steps up to the lectern to make a long-winded introduction. "I'd like to tell you about the most important, fascinating, earth-shattering person who ever existed. He's changed the shape of history. He's influenced kings, princes, popes, and czars. He's made his mark in literature, music, art, philosophy, theology. And here to talk about him is my good friend Joe." Yuck, yuck, big laugh. *Here to talk about Jesus was my good friend, Mr. Spiritual Director.*

"So what have you decided to do about your career?" he asked.

"I'm feeling better about what I do," I said.

"Really? I thought you weren't happy. I thought you wondered what God wanted you to do."

"I did. But I really like this job now." For the time being I *was* happier. I'd found a writing job at a magazine. "I get to write. I get to read a lot about God. I get to talk to interesting people. Sometimes I daydream about God."

"Glad to hear it. Have you ever seen that movie *Chariots of Fire?*"

I nodded my head, chomping on a peanut.

"There's a scene in it where the young man who's going to be a missionary, Eric Liddall, I think"—the minister was back—"is walking with his sister in the hills of Scotland. And yes, he tells her, he does plan on going to China and doing what God calls him to do, but first he's going to run in the Olympics, because, he says—and this is a wonderful phrase—'When I run, I feel God's pleasure.'"

"I remember that."

"Whatever you do, look for that. You're doing the Lord's work if you feel God's pleasure."

We went into the dining room, where he had pasta and I ordered shepherd's pie. We spoke of architecture, art, and the rotting beams in his church's apse. We talked about the books that lined the club's walls and a few of the paintings. (I was struck with an acute case of lust for a New England landscape.) And then he became very sincere. He looked at me straight on with his lapis lazuli eyes. "You will be very successful," he said.

How did he know?

"People like you are successful," he added, which made me wonder what kind of people I was.

After dessert we stood up. I brushed away the bread crumbs that always fell on my lap and set my crumpled napkin beside my plate like a trophy. We walked to the red-carpeted landing and shook hands. His parting words were, "Never stop praying. Each day you'll learn something new."

That was that. He sent me on my way. I almost wished he'd patted me on the head, like the Grinch patting Cindy Lou Who ("who was only two") on her nearly hairless Dr. Seuss head. I felt unprepared to meet the world. What about therapists? What about shrinks? What about twelve-step support groups? Weren't you supposed to need them forever? Weren't you in perpetual recovery? Wouldn't I always need a spiritual director?

I took the carpeted stairs two by two, pushed the polished brass handle of the front door, and walked out into the din of midtown. What now? What about all the unresolved problems in my life? Where would guidance come from now? Who would hear about my prayers? Who would interpret them? Would I even say them if I knew no one was going to give me a regular checkup?

The next morning I was standing as usual on the subway platform. I had a brand-new copy of *Vanity Fair* in my brief-case, wafting waves of fragrance from the perfume ads I hadn't yet ripped out. I had the urge to coddle myself with the current events of life's vanity fairs, as forgettable as the lyrics to last year's hit song. I could start out the day by catching up on a scandal, indulging my envy of the rich and famous, searching for details to support my moral superiority. Or I could take out the small green-bound Gideon volume of the New Testament and psalms.

Three psalms, that had been my recipe. Then silence. Listening for God.

I hesitated for a moment; then, giving in to some internal prompting, I turned to the psalms. I was into the meditative habit. It was too late. I was hooked on morning prayer. *Vanity Fair* would have to wait. (And don't think for a moment that I didn't read it later.)

It's the same way a college student goes to the library with his textbook, knowing that the place itself with its quiet, books, and other students will inspire him to study. Or the way a salesman who could never gather the pluck and charisma to make aggressive calls from home finds inspiration at his desk, not far from the water-cooler gossip. A place and time can trigger the desire to pray. I've trained myself to use the subway like that.

The distant rumble of the approaching train, the rustle of my neighbors' newspapers, the sight of someone looking at a

Bible or fingering a rosary—these are my signals to resume my own spiritual journey. I've worked at making this place sacred for me. That means overlooking the smell of urine, the bum with his plastic bag of cans, the rowdy high school kids, the neighbor who wants to banter about the weather. Like the mental distractions that constantly intrude when I'm focusing on the divine, they are banished. When I'm finished and I open my eyes, I might just see the beauty behind the nasty headlines or the homeless man. Right now I need to pray.

I close my eyes and I'm jogging on my weekend loop, up along the rows of art deco buildings with old ladies sitting in the sun in aluminum chairs, their Caribbean caretakers next to them. Up through the park past picnickers who've decorated a copper beech in pink and blue crepe paper for a child's birthday party. "Quiet Zone" says a sign, and beneath it music on a boombox blares. I leap over a six-pack of empty beer bottles and run around a pile of trash that's been picked out of a can by a beggar in search of booty. On top of the hill is the Cloisters museum, filled with stones from crumbling medieval monasteries, the hewn blocks taken down, marked, boxed, and shipped from Europe, reassembled above the Hudson in a simulacrum of holiness. Somehow, even in the antiseptic environment, real holiness can be felt. The prayers repeated behind those stones for hundreds of years seem to echo in my ears whenever I pass. Sometimes I think of Thomas Merton, who spent boyhood years in France not far from the original site of one stripped cloister.

Now this subway train is my cloister, hallowed by the prayers I've said here as I stand with my hand around a cold metal pole or sit in a warm orange seat. The closing doors are my call to worship, the conductor's voice on the loudspeaker calling out the stops like the announcement of Sunday morning hymns.

I've been amazed at how prayer can transform a place, even a place as uninviting as a subway. I've seen the same thing happen on the fifteen blocks that go from my apartment to the teeming, overcrowded city hospital where my two sons were born. Both boys were born in late winter, when the streets had none of the promise of early spring, only the gray, grungy, garbagey stench of unchanging damp days and diesel exhaust from city buses hanging in the air. The route winds past neat bodegas, plantain vendors, rap-screaming radios, greasy pizzerias, Laundromats, discount clothing stores, and check-cashing outfits with bullet-proof windows. Drug dealers linger on corners, and the down-and-out try to coax coins from suburbanite drivers by threatening to wash their car windows with filthy rags (blackmail, really). And yet that stretch of Broadway reminds me of the prayers of thanks I said in passing, rushing to hold a newborn, filled with the joy of new life. Prayer has made it sacred.

On the subway I say the same prayers over and over again. Even now I say them. *God, I wish you'd give me a little bit more money. God, I'd give you such pride if I had just a little bit more cash. Think of all that I could do for the poor.* (My own transparent attempts at blackmail.) *Dear Lord, I'm tired of behaving like a jerk all the time. Why can't I be a little nicer? Why can't I be kinder? Okay, okay, I'll forgive the bastard, but you've got to forgive me. Okay?*

How I must bore God to tears with my repetition. He's heard it all before. He's heard it from people worthier than I.

He's heard it from me before. But all this talk, all this vain banter, all this praying with words is just a prelude so that I can go beyond words. So that it will simply be my needs doing the praying. That's where I really need help. You can try very hard at expressing just what you think God wants to hear from you, but your jealous, angry, or hurt self will speak up very quickly and show that you're not a saint.

The first crisis I had to handle without my spiritual director came when a friend let me down in a big way. Whether through flakiness or malicious intent or maybe jealousy, he messed up.

(I feel odd putting it down on paper, even in general terms, because to forgive is to forget, and to write about what has been forgiven is to pick at old wounds. Worse yet, cloaking the ill deed in a veil of secrecy—alluding to it without giving the details—makes it seem so unforgivable it can't be named. It *could* be named. It could be described in intimate detail in a family magazine without exciting any censors. But I choose not to name it. I'd rather not go into it, thank you very much.)

When my friend did me this disfavor, I wanted to forgive. I wanted to forgive very badly. I wrote a note masking my hurt with good humor, making my anger look charming so that he could still approach me without embarrassment. I made a few telephone calls, speaking into his answering machine, keeping up the jocular, jovial attitude. I knew about therapy. I knew I needed to express my anger openly, lest it turn against me and attack me like a worm eating the insides of an apple, making it rotten to the core; so I expressed my anger in a disarming way. But really, I wanted painfully, desperately to forgive. And I was never given the chance. I was never allowed to communicate the magnanimous words I had rehearsed to myself. All those short tries into a telephone answering machine were useless. My calls went unreturned, my letters unanswered.

When I walked by my friend's apartment, I was tempted to drop in unexpectedly. I imagined running into him in the street. His eyes would look away. Given enough warning, he would cross the avenue and hide in an ATM line at a bank. "Don't worry," I'd say, seeking him out. "It was nothing. I've gotten over it. I forgive you." I'd be the star of the colloquy, Lady Bountiful passing out indulgences. (There's nothing so damned self-righteous as goodness that hasn't said its prayers.)

For weeks I continued to rehearse the fantasy I'd been acting out. Eyes closed, I practiced to myself the right expression of forgiveness. How kind I would be, how accepting.

As the months passed, my playacting diminished. The initial sting of the wrong done was gone, leaving behind only bewilderment. Then I began to see myself more clearly. I was a phony. Had I forgiven my friend? Had I *really*? No. In fact, I hadn't done a darn thing. Instead, I had only tortured him (in my imagination) with my bigheartedness. I had wished for him to squirm in the presence of my wonderful kindness. I had made myself the star of the scene, both the victim and the hero.

This is the key to one of Christ's crucial messages. Pride is a deadly sin, and the pride of self-righteousness is the very worst, because it doesn't see itself for what it is. That's what I had found in that frustrating tale of the prodigal son. I had identified with the stay-at-home brother. He's the helpless one. He's the one most in need of God's forgiveness and love. I knew I couldn't get beyond the wrongs done me, except through prayer. "Forgive us our trespasses as we forgive those who trespass against us." It *is* a two-way street.

Strolling down that two-way street on the subway, I could finally forgive. And really forget. Get on with it. If by some golden chance I were to run into my friend, I would be able to greet him with unaffected honesty and delight.

He *did* eventually get in touch with me. Maybe God worked through him. At a moment of distress he called. First he spoke to Carol, addressing himself to the matter at hand. And then he spoke to me. I didn't have any trouble saying, "I've missed you. It's been a long time. I'm glad you called." There was no rancor. I didn't have to be self-conscious about my voice, wondering how it sounded, wondering if it wavered. I meant what I said. That's a miracle of prayer, the work of God reaffirming who we are, giving us authenticity, making our words true.

Here on the subway I repeat the same prayer over and over again until I can get it right. *Forgive us our trespasses as we forgive those who trespass against us*, except that I usually say it in the Presbyterian version of my childhood, using the word *debts* instead of *trespasses. Forgive us our debts as we forgive our debtors.* I'll probably never get it right, but I try. Prayer is the only earthly endeavor where trying is enough.

My eyes are closed, and the train shakes as it rounds a curve. I clutch the green-bound Bible in my hands. The man next to me falls asleep. Suddenly his head falls on my shoulders. I open my eyes as he jerks his head up and apologizes.

"That's okay," I say, thinking, *I forgive you.*

I'm back on the subway on a warm spring evening, riding home on the crowded rush-hour train. I picture my wife at home cooking dinner—peeling the carrots or punching soda crackers into the meatloaf—and I'm filled with thankfulness for all the good things God has given me. I can imagine my children sprawled on the floor, plotting elaborate battles with their plastic knights and castles. Soon I'll get home and take them to the park to toss a ball or climb the jungle gym, and later I'll read to them the exploits of the children in the Narnia chronicles or the myths of the Greek gods. I'll sing them their goodnight song and hear their prayers; then Carol and I will have adult conversation about the book she's writing and what happened at the office today and what movies were reviewed today.

Overwhelmed with the goodness of life, intoxicated by the spring air (even in the A train), delighted by the murky shape of my life, I can barely concentrate on the paperback book I'm reading. I'm hardly aware of the surge of commuters around me, the doors slamming open and shut, the conductor calling out the station stops. I close my eyes in a deep satisfaction that's like prayer.

The next thing I know, someone is slugging me in the face, a cold fist hitting my nose and cheek. I duck my head; the fist comes again. I cover my face with my book. Blood drips onto Tolkien. My fellow passengers scramble to get away from the guy who's hitting me, and someone shouts, "What the . . . ?" Echoing that thought, I stagger to my feet, still hiding my head, and dart out the opened door in the company of several others. My nose is sore and bloody; I'm in a daze. The doors close, separating me from whoever it was, and the train disappears from the platform.

"It looked like a Hispanic guy," one man tells me on the platform. "You should make a report."

"He's still on the train," another observer says.

"There's a police station right here," an undercover straphanger says, and I stagger past a glossily painted orange concrete-block wall into an unmarked underground office right out of Perry Mason, radios crackling, phones ringing. A couple of uniformed cops, their extra bulk hanging over their black belts, ask me questions, and a prim secretary types my answers on a manual typewriter (a typewriter!). Was there any motive? Did you see who hit you? Had he been drinking? What was he wearing? What did he look like? What time was this? Are you in shock? Then one of the guys, taking my measured answers in stride, tells me off the record that I look like a prosecutor. Am I an attorney? No, I'm not. Well, at any rate, they decide to get an ambulance for me. "We'll have them take you to Presbyterian. You'll feel more comfortable there than at Harlem Hospital." (They're trying to tell me it was a racially motivated incident.)

First I call Carol. "Don't worry," I say. "I'm all right. Somebody hit me on the subway."

"Are you really all right?" she asks.

"I think so. Maybe my nose is broken." I can hear her take a deep breath. "Start dinner without me. It'll probably be a while."

I'm whisked away by ambulance, sirens blaring, from 145th Street to 168th Street, and I sit for hours on the hard plastic seats in the emergency waiting room with mostly Dominican immigrants, their feverish children sleeping in their laps, older siblings playing portable video games beneath the fluorescent glare. Nurses look up from clipboards; cashiers behind bullet-proof glass take money and promises to pay; a beefy security guard fiddles with the handcuffs jangling on his thigh.

By now I feel no anger, only bewilderment. Maybe the cops were right. Maybe I had the wrong shade of skin that day on a multicolored train (though I wasn't the only male with lighter skin). Maybe I reminded my crazed attacker of some teacher who had flunked him. Maybe the guy just wanted my seat. If he wanted my jacket, he could have asked. I started to feel a little proud. A certifiable victim of crime, I had the marks of the twentieth century on me—plus a first-rate shiner and a slightly modified nose. I sailed through triage, was X-rayed, then waited some more. Finally, at about 10:00 P.M., a doctor told me that my nose wasn't broken but would probably swell up before it went down. Released, I was back on the streets. I walked the fifteen blocks home.

"Rick, you've got to be more careful than you are in the city," a friend warned. "You've got to guard your flank and keep your wits about you at all times." *Thanks all the same,* I thought—and I still think. I'd rather not. Life is too short to live in fear. *Perfect love casteth out fear.* I'm careful, I'm not foolhardy, but there are certain blows you can't shield yourself from. Fists can come out of anywhere. You can't hide all the time. You can only live the best you know how and trust that your faith will help you through the dark tunnels and unexpected knockouts.

The bruises bloomed like a Christmas poinsettia and then faded. Life went on. A kid at work volunteered to track down my assailant and beat him up. I said I'd pass. My prayer life went on. I'm a little less oblivious on subway trains, but I'm not afraid of taking the A train at 11:00 P.M. after going to the theater or the rush-hour local past 145th Street. I suppose the only real casualty was Tolkien. I've never had the urge to finish volume two of the trilogy (the drops of dried blood dissuade me). The prayerful state I was in at the time of the attack was interrupted, but prayers are always interrupted. And then they resume. They can continue even when the rest of life is going on about them.

There's a Henry James story about two well-known artists, one a painter and the other a writer. They're vacationing in Switzerland, going on picnics, hiking, and talking—mostly talking interminably, as people do in Henry James stories— when the narrator notices something odd about the writer. Wherever he might be—on the veranda, in the hotel lobby, at the dining room table, back in his room—his real self is working furiously on his writing. On the other hand, the painter, a brilliant conversationalist, doesn't really exist unless someone is around to hear him speak. He's like the moon, incapable of generating his own light, able only to bask in another's glow.

When I first read this story, my greatest fear was that I would end up like the brilliant conversationalist, that I wouldn't really exist unless I was providing company for others. I wouldn't exist on my own. I could never be alone. I thought that maybe I'd have to become a great artist to savor solitude.

I don't feel that way anymore. My work on prayer has given me that quiet room in the back of my head (or maybe at the bottom of my soul)—that space where I'm furiously working at growing in spite of life's interruptions and setbacks. In the midst of making phone calls, filling out forms for the PTA, taking cash out of the ATM, or being beaten up on the subway, my best self can be back home in my prayer closet. (A closet case!) If I can give God a good ten minutes of my morning, he'll give me the rest of the day. *Keep me as the apple of the eye, hide me under the shadow of thy wings.* I don't mind losing myself in busywork as long as my real self, my deepest self, is concentrated in the regenerating pleasures of the soul. *The Lord is nigh unto all them that call upon him, to all that call upon him in truth.*

So where is *your* prayer closet? Where is *your* quiet place? Don't look for the mountaintop with a magnificent view. You want a spot where you'll be encouraged to look inward. I read once in a handbook of advice for writers that a writer should choose a room in the house where she won't be distracted. She should look for a place with a limited vista—a garden wall, a corner of sky, a few trees, a bush in the backyard. A dramatic view of snow-topped mountains and singing pines can be too much. Just a bit of foreground is enough. So too in prayer: look to the blades of grass or the lichen on a rock. Observe the pill bug hiding under a leaf or the impatiens dripping out of the redwood planter; then close your eyes. Look inward.

I love the beach for praying. You can lie on the sand near the ocean and close your eyes, and even if you're on Coney Island in August you can feel quite alone; the sound of the waves on the shore drowns out all other noise. You can't hear the couple arguing next to you, and the radio blasting near the lifeguard station seems miles away. All sounds are smothered by the ocean's white noise. On a busy, blanketed beach I've often felt utterly alone—in the world but not of the world. It's almost like being on a crowded rush-hour subway train.

Here I am, back on the A train, thankful for the click-clack of the wheels on the track, the rumble of the car in a dark tunnel, the roar of the accelerating train. There's the old lady praying with her rosary and the young Orthodox Jewish man with his beard and prayer book. Out of the corner of my eye I can tell that the black girl sitting next to me is looking at my Bible and me. I try to ignore her, fearful that she will interrupt to tell me about her Wednesday night Bible study group and her church . . . perhaps I'd like to come? *No, I wouldn't,* I tell myself even before I've been invited. I want this precious time alone, that's all.

"Is that your Bible?" she asks. A ridiculous question. Who else's would it be?

"Yes," I say tentatively.

"I forgot mine. I usually read it on my way to work."

"Would you like to borrow mine?"

"Thank you."

I close my eyes, knowing that I'm with a silent minority of people at work.